The Question
of Value

Thinking through
Nietzsche, Heidegger,
and Freud

James S. Hans

Southern Illinois University Press
Carbondale and Edwardsville

For Allen,

Master of the Buccal Dance

Copyright © 1989 by
The Board of Trustees,
Southern Illinois University
All rights reserved.
Printed in the United States of America
Designed by Barbara J. King
Production supervised by Natalia Nadraga
92   91   90   89   4   3   2   1

Library of Congress Cataloging-in-Publication Data

Hans, James S., 1950–
    The question of value

    Bibliography: p.
    1. Values. 2. Nietzsche, Friedrich Wilhelm, 1844–1900—Influence.
3. Heidegger, Martin, 1889–1976—Influence. 4. Freud, Sigmund,
1856–1939—Influence.
    I. Title.
BD232.H296 1989   121'.8   88-18451
ISBN 0-8093-1506-8

The paper used in this publication meets the minimum requirements of
American National Standard for Information Sciences
—Permanence of Paper for Printed Library Materials,
ANSI Z39.48-1984. ♾

Contents

Preface

I should begin by stating what this book *is not*. It is *not* a scholarly or critical study of Nietzsche, Heidegger, or Freud. Indeed, for a book with those names in the title, this text makes few references to them, particularly to Heidegger and Freud. I make no claim here for either a thorough or an accurate reading of the works of any of these writers. Instead, I seek to work out of a space that they opened up. In choosing to think through them, I do not pretend to be using their eyes; I am using my own. In the first chapter, for example, I more or less dispense with the question of Being and beings, a thought Heidegger believed to be the most essential. I do not deny that this was an important notion for Heidegger; rather, I simply assert that the language through which such questions are phrased is so hopelessly compromised today that one must put the entire matter into abeyance. The question of Being may have been of central importance to Heidegger, but it seems to me to be a concern that takes us away from the issues of greatest significance.

I seek to think through Nietzsche only to the extent that this book is an extended reflection on the world that he presented us with, a world in which the questions of temporality and revenge are paramount. I make use of Heidegger because I believe that his hermeneutic method of thinking is in itself an attempt to abjure the spirit of revenge. Likewise, Freud is an important part of this book because his discussion of the death instinct and the pleasure principle has everything to do with the human couplet of time and revenge. I think through these writers simply because it is impossible not to when one is concerned with the question of human value.

The focus of *The Question of Value*, then, is not on the writers whose names are given in the subtitle but on the idea of the main title, or the question of value. We know that Nietzsche was the first writer to use the word *value* in its modern sense, but our current discourse seems to have forgotten that Nietzsche's great critique was finally devoted to destroying the idols so that new values could take over the space that they occupied. Indeed, Nietzsche asserts this again and again, telling us in *The Gay Science* that he believes "that the weights of all things must be determined anew," and proclaiming in *On the Genealogy of Morals* that "*all* the sciences have from now on to prepare the way for the future task of the philosophers: this task understood as the solution of the *problem of value*, the determination of the *order of rank among values*." Our current critical discourse pays a great deal of obeisance to Nietzsche, yet one hears very little about the question of value anymore, even if for Nietzsche it was the central problem.

It could be argued that critiques of the older values are an essential part of our attempts to determine the new weights of things, and Nietzsche's own work would be a primary example of how this can be the case. Any "deconstruction" of the old idols works toward the establishment of new values in some ways, and so such work is to be commended. But one must wonder, finally, if our present "deconstructions" are as useful as they might seem. There can be no doubt that writers like Jacques Derrida have performed brilliant critiques of the older system of values, but at the same time their work seems to be infected by the same kind of absolutism they are intent on destroying. As has been pointed out before, Derrida seems so completely disgusted by his inability ever to escape the clutches of the metaphysic intrinsically connected to the words we all must use that he seems willing to settle for a kind of endless dance around the "corruption" of the signs he must perforce employ. But if it is true that our language cannot escape the metaphysic upon which it is based, it does not follow that we can do no more than endlessly point to the ways our signs are dependent on a system we have rejected. As Derrida himself has insisted, the crucial question is not whether or not we can escape our complicity in metaphysical language—we cannot—but rather how we proceed once we are aware of that fact. In *The Question of Value* I take the position that we must move in a different direction with that knowledge, that it is not enough simply to hover at the edge of the metaphysical abyss.

The problem of value as it presents itself to us today can be expressed in several ways. As a result of Nietzsche's own apocalyptic tendencies, we remain caught in a mode of discourse that seems all too binary: we reject the premises of the system in which we are presently caught and conjure some "rough beast" of a future that will be irretrievably different from what we know now. By placing the rough beast at the end of the line, as Derrida does in "Structure, Sign, and Play in the Discourse of the Human Sciences" and elsewhere, we have in effect abjured the middle ground where we find ourselves. We have committed ourselves to a set of values so totally "other" than the ones we presently have that we have been able to avoid the question of value altogether. Again, this is another form of absolutism that allows us to proceed with the critique of the past without seriously addressing how we as humans make value every day. In specifically raising the question of value as I do here, I hope to redirect our attention to the obvious fact that whatever rough beast appears in the future will come from the values we are in the process of establishing today.

More importantly, the very idea that any new system must be a rough beast, I would argue, is a ruse in itself. Our distress over the loss of our old idols has led us to *assume* that any new conception of values must be radically other, but this does not necessarily follow at all. It may be that we shall end up with something that today remains unrecognizable, but it may just as well be that we end up with a system of values that looks very much like the one we have today, with the crucial difference of our embodied, finite status in the world at the center of it rather than our desire to escape from the finitude we have been fighting against for millennia. We simply do not know the answer to such questions at the moment, and the only way to begin to address them is by starting out from where we are at present and assessing the value of things as we see them.

Thus, instead of a scholarly or critical study, what I offer here is a speculative essay, an essay in which the question of value is repeatedly raised in different contexts in an attempt to focus on the present moment and the values that we are in the process of working through even as we continue our critique of the past. My vision of a speculative essay, however, involves a methodological problem that must also be addressed here. True to my own understanding of the tradition that comes out of Nietzsche and Heidegger, I do not provide a sustained, reasoned argument in the following pages. In one sense, the very point of the book is that reasoned argument in the traditional sense is also a ruse. Heidegger made the same point repeatedly, so there is nothing new in that notion. Still, we remain accustomed to a distinction between assertion and argument that I have ignored in my discussion. For the most part, what I say is nothing more than assertion, if you will; I provide no "arguments" for what I state because I believe that the "argument"—or the "reasons"—is inherent in the coherence of the principles upon which my assertions are based. In this sense, my book is not an attempt to persuade anyone to see the world differently on the basis of a series of carefully reasoned arguments. On the contrary, I present a way of looking at and thinking about the question of value that rises or falls with the adequacy of its mode of questioning. There is always a danger in such a method, for it fundamentally denies the power of reason to bring us to the conclusions we need, but then the belief in the power of reason is even more dangerous from the vantage point presented here.

I can phrase this matter in one more way: my "method" is related to the hermeneutic circle as Heidegger understood it. It is "recursive" in the sense that each chapter proceeds through a series of questions that circle around to various junctures where they come together. Certain fields of thought are thereby established through which we can begin to determine a pattern of more viable responses to the world of which we are a part. In this sense the hermeneutic circle is little different from the mode employed by Socrates in the dialogues. The "argument" here is not linear; the circles are endless, but one would hope that they accrete more value every time one goes around them.

In the end, the question of value always occurs in the midst of the embodied world in which we find ourselves, and it is always essentially a question of how we value *time*. As Nietzsche repeatedly stated, we are nihilists because we loathe our essentially temporal natures, and the assertion of a new set of values can take place only when we learn to affirm what we most fully are, temporal creatures. In seeking to redirect our inquiries to the question of value, I am arguing that too much of our best present work still remains driven by the human revulsion against time, but more importantly I am contending that we are at least capable of beginning to establish a new series of values on the basis of an affirmation of what we are. We have been in the midst of this question for a century now, and only our continuing desire to bring back the old world of the timeless idols has kept us from seeing how much we have already begun to weigh the value of things anew.

Acknowledgments

This book is dedicated to Allen Mandelbaum, a tutelary spirit whose presence in my life and work has made all the difference. From my graduate-school years to the present, he has been there to guide, encourage, and inspire with his intellect, his generosity, and his care. There are relatively few people in a life of whom one can say that without them one would not have become what one is, but I have no doubt that without Allen Mandelbaum, my work would have never been possible. I hope that *The Question of Value* conveys in its own way the generosity of spirit that he has passed on to me.

Herbert Lindenberger has also contributed in important ways to the development of my work, and I am grateful for his encouragement and support. Michael McCanles and Murray Krieger are to be thanked for their assistance at various crucial points in my career; Ronald Sharp has been a valued friend and interlocutor for years; and Myrddin Jones has regularly reminded me of the need for a craftsman's attention to detail. Robert Hedin and Gillian Overing have been the kind of friends and colleagues one could not do without; they have always been there when I needed them, and our dialogues over the years have often helped me to clarify my ideas and added to my understanding of the issues upon which my work is focused. Dillon Johnston and Robert Lechner have supported my efforts in any number of ways, and I thank them. I am also appreciative of the congenial environment Wake Forest University continues to provide for me. Curtis Clark has been my editor at Southern Illinois University Press, and I am grateful for his contribution to the publication of this book.

In earlier books I have attempted to suggest the manifold ways in which my wife, Hilma, has added to the quality of my work (and life), so I can only add here that she has aided me most by so fully affirming what she is. My daughter, Heather, was born after this manuscript was written, but there is no one in my life who more acutely brings into focus the question of value and the burden of temporality than her, and I am thankful for her rich presence.

Finally, chapter 1 of this book was previously published in somewhat different form as "The Question of Value in Nietzsche and Heidegger," in *Philosophy Today*, vol. 28, no. 4/ 4 (Winter 1984), pp. 283–99, and I should like to thank the journal for permission to reprint it here.

The Question
of Value

1 The Lyrical Nature
of the Question

Questions have always been at the heart of any philosophical enterprise just as they are the locus of all important activity in any other cultural domain. They frame the context of the unknown or inexplicable and at the same time provide us with a basis for making sense out of that which stymies us. We all ask questions as a matter of course, most of the time without even recognizing that we are doing so. Likewise, linguists and philosophers have regularly inquired about the various kinds of questions we raise, attempting either to enumerate the categories through which they can be understood or to demonstrate to which aspect of our world the questions apply. My concern here will be a much narrower one, as I wish to analyze the mode of questioning that has become more prominent over the last hundred years in such thinkers as Nietzsche and Heidegger. In one sense there is nothing new in the way Nietzsche or Heidegger asks questions; indeed, Heidegger would simply tell us that he is returning to a much older way of raising issues, one first traced by the pre-Socratics and found in the Socratic dialogues as well. But if he is forced to go back to the pre-Socratics for a model, he must surely be doing something considerably different from traditional academic philosophy. And he is, as the various attitudes toward him as a philosopher suggest.

While I am more interested in a mode of questioning than in a specific critique of Heidegger's or Nietzsche's work, the two men provide a good point of focus because opinion is so divided about them and because it seems time to ask what can and cannot be done with their modes of inquiry. Traditional Anglo-American philosophy finds their work to be philosophical in the weakest of senses because it makes little use of the analytic tools that are available to the two writers: logical approaches to their arguments yield little, and no claims to reason are made that could be said to be universally reproducible. When Heidegger ends one of his essays on Nietzsche by telling us that "thinking begins only when we have come to know that reason, glorified for centuries, is the most stiff-necked adversary of thought," we must assume that he is not glorifying reason and so cannot be precisely evaluated by its terms ("The Word of Nietzsche," in *The Question Concerning Technology and Other Essays*, trans. William Lovitt [New York: Harper and Row, 1977], p. 112). For traditional philosophers, both Heidegger and Nietzsche seem more to resemble the rhapsode in the *Ion* than Kant carefully delineating the nature of the analytic and synthetic. Similarly, many of the etymologies Heidegger bases his work on—both Greek and German— seem all too similar to the fanciful lineages Socrates makes use of in the *Cratylus*, and this makes his work equally suspect.

More importantly, though, there is the question of whether or not one can make any use of the approaches Nietzsche and Heidegger employ. It may be true, for example, that philosophers like Hegel projected a utopian end to their thought that we no longer countenance, but they also developed systems that could be analyzed and evaluated. The same cannot be said for Nietzsche and Heidegger. Nietzsche will regularly proclaim the coming of a change, but his manner of doing so seems to many to be far too unsystematic to be of any help to us, particularly when the definitive text, *The Will to Power*, was never finished and remains in fragmentary form. Heidegger never specifically heralds any utopian ends in his work, but he seems to spend his whole life hovering around the relationship between Being and beings and suggests to many that his ideas are based on a return to the Eden of pre-Socratic thought. In both cases, even if we concede that there is much that is fruitful, many would argue that there is no way to make use of the insights lodged in such nonanalytical texts. The scions of progress would say that what is being practiced in such work is a Western brand of Eastern quietistic philosophy, and texts like Heidegger's *Discourse on Thinking* would seem to confirm this. Even if these accusations are finally absurd, though, we still need to ask what future directions for philosophy and Western culture are open to us if we are to take Nietzsche and Heidegger seriously and if we are to assume that they are doing something different through their mode of questioning that is worth pursuing in ways that have not yet been explored.

If we return to the rhapsode in the *Ion*, we can get a clearer sense of what is at stake, for Ion's manner of reciting poetry is one of the crucial issues in the debate. It is no accident that Heidegger's work intersects the domain of the poetic, or that he regularly relies on poets like Hölderlin and Trakl, any more than it is an accident that Nietzsche's "aphoristic" form bears close resemblance to a way of writing poetry. Unlike the logicians who seek to keep philosophy neat and clean, Heidegger and Nietzsche dirty the waters by conflating categories and writing texts that are neither philosophy nor poetry. In effect, their work denies the carefully established framework for philosophical speculation that has been developed over the past few hundred years and undermines the value of the analytic method. But if we assume that they are nevertheless serious philosophers—rather than simply rejecting out of hand what they have done—we need to ask why they so studiously ignore the boundary between the aesthetic and the philosophical, why they insist upon merging the two in the striking ways they do.

Nietzsche and Heidegger base their work on lyrical questions. They unite the epistemological and the aesthetic and begin from that vantage point. Inasmuch as we have done our best to keep truth and beauty separate, however, this is an unorthodox strategy to employ. What is to be gained by asking lyrical questions? Why not leave that to the poets? Or perhaps we could ask the question the other way: why is it appropriate for Yeats to ask how we can know the dancer from the dance while it is inappropriate for Heidegger to ask what it means for language to be the house of Being? Inasmuch as Heidegger thinks that language calls to us, and that Being is allowed to emerge through the calling of language through us, is it not possible that his questions *should* be lyrical? There is a great philosophical divide at this point. Heidegger does not see the traditional form of questioning as leading to any kind of knowledge or understanding; rather, it seems only to contribute to the accretion of a certain kind of information—about the truth or falsity of this or that statement, this or that argument. No knowledge is gained; only specific pieces of data are verified or rejected. But Heidegger's kind of question often is too personal—too lyrical—to yield reproducibility, so the knowledge gained is not general but particular, and while it may have value for other people, it always remains tied to its original context. Only the mode of questioning itself has general value, and it begins with the assumption that the aesthetic and the epistemological belong together, that all questions of fundamental importance are essentially lyrical in nature.

Both Heidegger and Nietzsche begin with the assumption that the epistemological and the aesthetic are inextricably connected—not that they *need* to be reconnected, for we have never been able to separate them in spite of repeated attempts to do so. We simply need to see how they are always found together. This move reverses the direction of modern philosophy, whose goal was to delineate specific categories for every human domain, but the reversal only assumes from the outset what analytic philosophers always had to concede in the end in any case. Every attempt to keep the true and the beautiful separate finally demonstrated how impossible it was to do so. Even more, one could say that the connection between the true and the beautiful was denied at the outset—in order to keep the true pure—while the goal was to recover their essential connection nonetheless. Because one began with their essential difference, one had to resort to paradoxical formulations at the limits of one's system. Thus, for example, Kant would construe the sublime as the limit point for his Ideas and Schiller would conceive of the aesthetic as the negation of the true and the good at the same time that it conjoined them with the beautiful. He would deny the connection of the good, the true, and the beautiful even as his goal was to show how the aesthetic was the location where the true, the good, and the beautiful came together.

Heidegger and Nietzsche, on the other hand, begin with the assumption that we always confront the true *only* when it is connected to the beautiful. Rather than trying to recover their moment of union, they begin with it as an assumption. If philosophy since Descartes has sought to banish the aesthetic to its own discrete domain, Heidegger and Nietzsche argue that one can only find the true in the company of the beautiful: the philosopher as rhapsode singing the emergence of Being into beings through language, as Heidegger would have it. But as Socrates made clear to Ion, this means that the philosopher is not reasonable; indeed, it suggests that he is mad. It also means, as Socrates pointed out, that the philosopher as rhapsode has no particular area of expertise—what he does he does while not in his right mind; what he says comes from outside of him and has nothing to do with a knowledge of that about which he is speaking. The lack of control involved in this mode of thinking is antithetical to our conceptions of the coldly analytic philosopher, and we tend to be troubled by what seems to be a risky enterprise: if the philosopher has no control, who can guarantee the results of his statements? These unsettling assumptions prompt us yet again to ask why Heidegger and Nietzsche begin with a series of premises that calls into question the philosophical nature of their work.

Why should philosophical questions be lyrical? *How* can they be lyrical? In Heidegger's case, we readily find the attention to wordplay, to the multiple meanings of words, to etymologies, and to language in general. In part, as with the etymologies of Greek words like *aletheia*, Heidegger has an almost sacred belief that words as they first emerged had a more salient set of meanings than they now have. Specific words are often kernels of truth that will reveal a great deal if only he can crack them in the right way and show what has been lost in their historical lives. Heidegger generally claims that he is simply listening to what the words have to say to him, as if he is not a dominant participant, and in this he may well be right, even if he does read more into his etymologies than many Greek scholars would countenance. There is, of course, the scholarly question of how accurate his etymologies are, but the more important question is what is made clear through them, regardless of their historical accuracy. It may, for example, be the case that the word *aletheia* has far less to do with unconcealedness than Heidegger says it does, and it may have even less to do with the various meanings of concealed and unconcealed that he derives from that, but the crucial point is the value of seeing the idea of truth from the vantage point of unconcealedness, and here Heidegger is extremely illuminating regardless of the scholarly value of his linguistic investigations.

Equally often, however, the words and the wordplay are more deliberately chosen, as in the use of *heissen* (to call or to name), which Heidegger regularly uses as a word that encapsulates much of his thinking. That he finds man called, commanded, by language; that he finds man called in the sense of having a mission; that calling brings forth the sense of voice that he finds so important; and that the act of naming is also related to this calling in various ways are certainly more important and less accidental in Heidegger's exposition of the meanings of *heissen* than any particular philological accuracy. There is no doubt that he treats words as a poet does, from his coinages to his penchant for drawing multiple meanings out of seemingly banal terms, but it is equally true that what he reveals in the process is significant, at least as relevant as the attitude toward language that he employs.

From Heidegger's perspective, one must be devoted to language and that which it reveals, and the devotion is central to the lyrical quality of his questions. Like the rhapsode, he puts himself under the control of language—"language speaks man"—and here we find the locus of a great many of the objections traditional philosophers have about his work. Heidegger begins with the assumption that he is not in control, that rather he is being led by language. His questions give him an orientation, but he in turn is led to where the question takes him. And certainly in a specific sense this does not lead to reproducibility of results, for language leads each of us in different ways according to our own contexts and orientations. But one can learn how to be led by language, and one of the yields of Heidegger's work is that he shows us again and again how to go about doing this.

To say, however, that language speaks man, or to agree to

be led by the force of language, is to raise far more difficult questions, the first of which is simply whether or not we are in fact spoken by language. Most of us would certainly like to think that we control our words rather than the other way around, but Heidegger suggests that this is merely an illusion on our part, akin to the belief that the sun travels around the earth. We instinctively rebel against such an idea and point immediately to the many situations where we can see that we are choosing our language and have control over it. The force of our personality may dictate much of our word choice, but that is far different than language speaking us. Or is it? If, for example, I were in a conversation with someone, and I wanted to tell the person something negative without bearing the brunt of his wrath, I would choose my words carefully. Instead of saying "That was a very foolish thing to do," I might be inclined to say something like "I don't understand why you did that." Normally I would assume that I was the one editing the various possibilities in my mind before I came up with such an innocuous formulation, but what part did language play in my editing process? Certainly it provided me with the various possibilities from which to choose, and in that sense I was responding to the nuances of language as much as I was deliberating about a social context.

At a different level, the issue becomes murkier. It is often the case that one instinctively chooses a word because it "feels" right, just as a poet must surely do. One can readily enough imagine Heidegger instinctively feeling that the word *heissen* was appropriate to what he was thinking about and only later, after exploring the possibilities of the word, discovering how much more appropriate it was to his concerns than he had ever imagined. We are back to the issue of the rhapsode here, the notion that a person is somehow not in his right mind when he falls upon words in this way and traces the consequences of their meanings. Heidegger's work certainly bears resemblance to the process of the rhapsode, and this is no doubt why he can so forcefully maintain that language speaks man. The rhapsode allows language to come to him, to speak through him, and his control over where it leads him is less than one might think. He is the subordinate partner in the relationship and recognizes that fact as much as Heidegger does. The glory and the music of the rhapsode's language convey the feeling of being overpowered by it, and certainly in the old days people saw such glory as the power of some divine force working within them.

Heidegger does not speak of language as a divine force, but he does say that language speaks man, and even that is too mystical for many. If we no longer believe that the gods inspire us when language captivates us, though, how are we to characterize such an experience? We can say that poets have overexcited nervous systems, or that they have a greater supply of noradrenaline in their bodies—we can come up with at least ten different ways of explaining the sense of inspiration, and they may all be right. Nevertheless, it is still the case that in such rhapsodic moments language speaks man. We can define the psychophysiological coordinates of the experience, we can explain it in any number of ways, but the language is still speaking the man. It is directing him rather than vice versa. It is true that the person so spoken is a participant in the process; it is true that the way in which language speaks him is dependent upon the psychological, cultural, linguistic and physiological contexts that the individual brings to the event; but it is equally true that language is speaking him, and that in some cases he is even surprised by what he discovers through his speaking.

A similar case could be made for our more mundane uses of language. To begin with, we seldom reflect upon our word choice—we let the words flow of their own accord until we are at a loss for them. Then we might sort through various possibilities until the right word presents itself, or we might try something else like leaving the subject alone in the hope that the word will come to us after we stop concentrating on its appearance. But how are these choices being made? Is our ego doing the choosing? Our personality? Our identity? One could argue so, but surely those concepts are at least as mysterious as the notion that language speaks man. We are simply more comfortable with the mystery of identity, so we say that our words are chosen on the basis of our inner being, which answers nothing inasmuch as no one knows exactly what such a creature is. But if we are willing to admit at least hypothetically that words like *ego* and *identity* are merely modern placeholders for mysteries about which we have no idea, we should also be willing to entertain the mysterious notion that language speaks man.

When Heidegger says that language speaks man, he is seldom referring to the kinds of examples I have discussed here. The specific cases in his work are rather a reflection of the way he lets language speak him within his essays. In general he is concerned with how Being is brought into presence through language via man. He is interested in showing how language, through the namings of man—which are a response to the call of Being—allows certain things to emerge into the foreground. A name calls attention to something, brings it out of the background, and as such reveals both a particular being and Being itself, inasmuch as Being is only present in particular beings. Man brings those things to the foreground that he finds interesting or dangerous or useful or striking in some other way, so language as it speaks him is always filtered through these contexts. Nevertheless, in the process of naming, Being and beings are revealed, and so is the nature of man, most specifically his naming abilities and his character as the shepherd of Being and language. I shall have more to say about this in a moment, but at present I want to probe why this conception sounds so strange to us and why we rebel against it so strongly.

To begin with, if language speaks man, we find our position in the world to be even less important than we thought. After Freud and Darwin and Copernicus, we thought we had seen it all, but then Heidegger comes along and tells us that we are not even the masters of our own language, that rather it masters us. This is demeaning enough, but it also comes to us at a time when we have lost sight of the nature of mastery as well. We have forgotten that mastery is a result of being mastered by something, by submitting to its discipline sufficiently to become a master. But if a poet is the master of his craft, surely he is so because he has submitted himself to the discipline of the language and been mastered by it. Only through such discipline will he be capable of listening properly to language, and the same can be said for all of us.

Our problems with mastery run deeper than that, though, and they return once again to confront the nature of the rhapsode: the rhapsode is not in his right mind, and we have placed our faith in reason. Given our total commitment to reason, we try to avoid situations that are not covered by it; we even try to act as if such situations do not exist. If the rules of reason do not apply, the irrational creeps in, and inasmuch as man has yet to learn adequately to distinguish the irrational that is nonetheless true from the irrational that is false, he is more inclined to throw out the rhapsode with the madman. In part this is why poets have become irrelevant—we do not want to say they are mad, but whatever they are, they are not reasonable, so the only thing left to do with them is to turn them into idle curiosities.

There are good reasons for our skittishness when it comes to the irrational, first because it is not always easy to discern the value of it and second because much of the evil we see in the world can be attributed to it. Hitler certainly was a rhapsode of sorts, and all too many people were willing to submit to the discipline of his mastery. This is a danger that never goes away, and it ought to make any person wary of the irrational, particularly when there are always enough smaller examples of such mastery around, from the rhapsodic powers of Jim Jones in a Guyanan jungle to the other cult figures that appear from time to time. Indeed, from one angle the problem is that all too many people are all too willing to submit to the mastery of another. We may be democratic in spirit, but not when in comes to giving everyone enough credit to discern the kinds of noxious power that result from submitting to this kind of discipline.

The problem of the mastery of people like Hitler is a real one, and no amount of argument can eliminate it from consideration. One could say, quite rightly, that many people submit to the Hitlers of the world because they want to avoid personal responsibility. One could say, quite rightly, that such discipline devoted to the sheer exercise of power and the desire to be master over others is also a misplaced sense of discipline and mastery. One could say any number of similar things, and they would all be true, but they do not diminish the possibilities for misunderstanding the appropriateness of discipline and mastery.

To say that language speaks man, and to suggest that man must be mastered by language, is nevertheless not to submit to the power of a Hitler. It is possible that a person could conceive of himself as being mastered by language and equally convinced that language has "told" him that he is the next savior of the world, but that is always possible in any case, regardless of whether or not an individual thinks that language masters him. It is also true that when one is genuinely mastered by language, the insights it leads one to can generate feelings of joy, which some people translate as power. A poet may experience this joy when he writes and realize that it has nothing to do with power over others, but he may not as well. The question is once again whether such misinterpretations are more likely to occur if one believes that language speaks man rather than that one has power over one's language. At the very least the humility involved in the former proposition might suggest that, if anything, one is more likely to realize the limits of one's power over language and others.

If we cannot easily eliminate the problem of discipline and mastery, we can at least recognize it and ask whether or not part of the difficulty comes from man's overblown sense of himself. Perhaps part of the problem is our sense of our autonomous egos doing battle in the world for power and status. By taking on such an autonomous role, we assume that we have more power to affect things than we do, and this in turn leads to abuses of power in its own right. Of course, the problems of power and its abuse were present long before the age of the autonomous individual—justified by the power of gods or kings—but there is no reason to assume that in accepting our subordinate position within the world we will necessarily fall under the sway of abusive powers. That language speaks man might be a blow to our egos, and this conception indeed raises problems that man has tried to ignore throughout his history, but inasmuch as we know those problems exist even as we try to ignore them, and inasmuch as we should know by now that reason does not resolve them and can even be put to use for their purposes, perhaps we should further investigate the possibilities of language speaking man, both despite the perils and because of them.

Part of the problem of reintroducing the connection between the aesthetic and the epistemological is that we cannot leave it at that. Both Nietzsche's and Heidegger's work show that one must also reintroduce the ethical, and that is where many of the difficulties arise. In one sense it is easy enough to concede the connection between the true and the beautiful—the true is often lyrical in nature, and in our everyday lives we have no trouble with that. But one cannot concede that connection without acknowledging that the good is irretrievably bound up in the equation as well. In a crucial way, both Nietzsche and Heidegger were essentially moral philosophers, and yet it is precisely the morality of their philosophies—or at least the possible consequences of them—that troubles us most. It is not simply that Nietzsche went mad or that Heidegger was seriously involved with fascism; it is rather that both of their philosophies raise problems we would prefer to avoid. It is one thing to say that Nietzsche's philosophy cannot legitimately be construed as a justification for fascism; it is another to say that we do not know what consequences follow from Nietzsche or Heidegger and are afraid to find out. And again, with some justification, for we have come to see reason as the last bastion of civilization, and without it to stand on, we are no longer sure of our ground.

The problem of Nietzsche and Heidegger is compounded further by the fact that their most insightful and illuminating readers are also misreaders of them. If Nietzsche and Heidegger seek a different conception of truth by reconnecting it to the aesthetic, their best readers construe them as eliminating the truth altogether and simply placing the aesthetic at the center of life: "The joyous affirmation of the freeplay of the world, and without truth" is Jacques Derrida's characterization of Nietzsche, and whereas this is accurate so long as one conceives of the truth as that static series of eternal verities man has always been longing for, all too often Nietzsche is misconstrued as joyously affirming nothing more than the power joyously to affirm, whether that power is put to good or bad use (Derrida, "Structure, Sign, and Play in the Discourse of the Human Sciences," in *The Structuralist Controversy*, eds. Richard Macksey and Eugenio Donato [Baltimore: Johns Hopkins University Press, 1972], p. 265).

Perhaps the most interesting commentary on the nature of the truth in Nietzsche comes from one of Heidegger's readings of him in *What Is Called Thinking?* There he tells us that Nietzsche's "true and one and only thought" is the following: *"For that man be delivered from revenge:* that is the bridge to the highest hope for me, and a rainbow after long storms" (*What Is Called Thinking?*, trans. Fred D. Wieck and J. Glenn Gray [New York: Harper and Row, 1972], p. 85). Heidegger sees this statement as an important mark on the pathway to thinking; implicitly and explicitly, he tells us that the spirit of revenge is the bar to all thinking and hence must be overcome, a strange conception when one considers that normally thinking and revenge have nothing to do with each other in our eyes. But he goes even further than that, explaining that this was Nietzsche's "true and one and only thought," again not the traditional view. Nietzsche does say here, however, that the bridge to his highest hope is that man be delivered from revenge, and we wonder why that should be so important. In the context of the passage in the "On the Tarantulas" section of *Thus Spake Zarathustra*, Nietzsche ties revenge to the desire for equality, against which he fights, and one can see how revenge operates in man's desire to bring his superiors down to his level. Nevertheless, that this should be the bridge to Nietzsche's highest hope and the passageway to the overman seems excessive. At the same time, it is the masterstroke of Nietzsche's work, for he sees here and elsewhere that mankind can only live with the essential connection between the aesthetic and the true if he is delivered from revenge—the only way to overcome the problems inherent in accepting the relationship between the true and the beautiful is to be able to live with their relationship to the good, and the only way to do that is to abjure the spirit of revenge.

Otherwise, the power of the will expends itself on the desire for revenge and seeks to master and subordinate to its own power and for its own resentful reasons the others who are the objects of resentment. Even more, Nietzsche says "that man be *delivered* from revenge"; he does not argue that man will deliver himself, suggesting that the power to be delivered from it comes not from man's conscious attempt to will himself over revenge, for that is really only another way of willing revenge itself. Rather, for Nietzsche only accepting the will to power makes it possible for man to be delivered from revenge.

The problem of revenge is deeper than that, however, as Heidegger shows when he quotes Nietzsche's definition of it: "This, yes, this alone is *revenge* itself: the will's revulsion against time and its 'It was' " (*What Is Called Thinking?*, trans. Fred D. Wieck and J. Glenn Gray [New York: Harper and Row, 1972], p. 93). Without going very much farther, Heidegger explains that our revulsion against time is the result of our reaction to its transitory nature; we find it difficult to accept the passing of time and hence rebel against its flow. Nietzsche sees our revulsion against time as the locus of our desire for revenge; a vengeful act both attempts to make amends for the time that has passed away and seeks to negate it, and while the act itself may be directed toward a specific event in one's life that one wishes to deny, in the end all acts of vengeance are devoted to overcoming time altogether. In this sense, an act of revenge becomes an attempt to stop time, to negate its power over one, to establish control over it, and the spirit of revenge for Nietzsche takes its roots here rather than in particular grievances against individuals.

But we do not simply have a revulsion against time; we are also rebelling against time's "It was," and whereas Heidegger wants to emphasize that the "It was" includes the now and the future—which it does—it more importantly gives a direction to the now and the future, and it is always a retrospective orientation. The revulsion against time and its passing away is always located within a specific "It was" that is most revolting, the individual's particular past time and the history that cannot be changed or overcome. The spirit of revenge is the will's attempt to undo what has already been done, to clean the slates and rectify the accounts, to negate the "It was" that seems to dominate the will in the present. The problem with our commitment to revenge, in both individual and cultural terms, is that it leads us to think that we can overcome and negate the past through an act of revenge, when in fact we only end up perpetuating the "It was" that so revolts us, leading in turn to the desire for further revenge. In this way, the acts of the will are always driven by the "It was" and reinforce the continuity of it that the act of revenge is supposed to break. Not only is the will opposing something against which it is always bound to lose; not only is the will in turn always directing its present actions in terms of a past that it wants—but will never be able—to overcome through revenge; but also each act of the will that arises out of the revulsion against the "It was" increases the revulsion and extends the power of the "It was" over the will. Every attempt to negate time is bound to fail, leading to greater frustration of our desires, prompting us one more time to commit an act that will once and for all eliminate the force of the "It was." In this way revenge perpetuates the endless series of blows that has regularly characterized man's attempt to overcome the passing away of time, which is his severest limit, and the result is that the spirit of revenge comes to be the defining characteristic of the will of man and of the revulsion he feels for himself.

The virtue of reason in traditional philosophy is that it is the tool that is supposed to be able to remove man from this endlessly vicious cycle of revenge, first because it is seen as an atemporal method—in taking man's consideration of his actions out of time and away from the "It was" that colors the will's choices in time, reason is supposed to clear the way for the overcoming of the will to revenge and its dominance over man's choices. In establishing reason as the mode of escape from revenge, however, philosophers also found it necessary to separate the true from the beautiful and the good, for the latter two are always context bound and inevitably connected to the "It was." If reason and its truths are to remain above the "It was," and to keep their purity, the beautiful and the good must be purged. In so doing, we think we have cleared a space away from the contingent that allows man to be reasonable and thus offers him a means of escape from the dominance of his revulsion against time.

The problem with establishing a pure, reasonable space is that the more this atemporal location is pursued, the smaller its space becomes. "Reason" moves from a generally viable human attitude that can be employed in the everyday world to a specific kind of method to test the viability of statements, and from there the method increasingly becomes purged of any particular contextual features, leading eventually to a set of assumptions that works but is more and more sterile because it has no applicability to the world in which people live. Likewise, philosophy itself increasingly becomes a discipline devoted to concerns that are irrelevant to life; its goal is rather to test assumptions, to attempt to fix things outside the flow of time. And it does so almost convincingly, but as it does, it loses any effectiveness it might have had to deal with a large part of its original purpose, which was to discern the nature of human existence and to deal with man's revulsion against the "It was."

Seen in this light, the emergence of so-called existential philosophies was a result of the failure of reason to deal with the will's revulsion against time and the concomitant desire for revenge. When everything reasonable had been done to help man overcome his revulsion, his revulsion remained; indeed, it had increased because reason itself had become the tool of revenge, the tool that attempted to negate and overcome the flow of time that so ruled man's will. In seeking to subdue the "It was," reason ended up making the spirit of revenge grow and expand its domain, for the belief in reason perpetuated and extended the notion that man is finally capable of overcoming the effects of time on his life. It became our most powerful tool of revenge even as it was committed to eliminating vengeance from our lives. This is why Heidegger is determined to explain that "reason, glorified for centuries, is the most stiff-necked adversary of thought." Not only has reason removed the true from the good and the beautiful, but in doing so it has removed itself from thinking as Heidegger conceives it. Not only has reason been unable to eliminate the revulsion of the "It was," it has made thought powerless to deal with revenge. Reason has sought to escape the "It was" by negating it, by denying it, by closing it off through reasonable means. In so doing, it has only avoided the problem and increased the spirit of revenge and eliminated the power of thinking.

Both Nietzsche and Heidegger turn toward a view of thinking that connects the true and the beautiful because they see that thought can only occur when it is aesthetic, when its lyrical qualities allow what is to emerge outside of the spirit of revenge that seeks to dominate and master and negate the passing of time. In making their questions lyrical, they demonstrate the necessity of bringing thought once again into the domain of the good. They also show how one can only begin to confront the spirit of revenge that dominates man and prevents him from seeing the lyrical nature of his world once one has reconnected thought to the question of value. If Heidegger is willing to say that language speaks man, and if he is willing to take the risk of being mastered by language, he can do so primarily because he knows that this is the only way he can be delivered from revenge. Put another way, we can say that if it is true that revenge is the revulsion of the will against time, one cannot escape that revulsion through reason, which is itself a part of the problem, as Nietzsche's thought of the eternal return makes clear. Only by accepting the possibility of the eternal return of the "It was" can one escape one's desire for revenge over it. Only by being mastered by the "It was" can one gain mastery of it, and one can only do that *within* the passing of time. This means that one must finally agree to think in the context through which one lives. To do so in turn means that one must accept that language speaks man, not simply because it always precedes and follows the existence of any person, but more importantly because it is the most powerful expression of the passing away of time, and only by submitting to the "It was" of language and letting it speak man can one escape the desire to use it for vengeful purposes. Language can certainly be used as an instrument of revenge just as one can argue that man speaks language, but both are expressions of the desire for the negation of the "It was."

Heidegger sees himself as on the way to thinking, and the fact that he always sees himself on the way raises another problem with the lyrical nature of his questions. Because he is always only on the way, he never seems to get anywhere. He always seems to be hovering on the threshold of Being and never seems to arrive. Like a good poem, his essays always open up more terrain and raise more questions than they resolve. The essential openness of his thinking leads some to say that he is not a philosopher at all, for philosophers are supposed to resolve at least some of the issues they raise. But the openness of the lyrical question—like the openness of Socrates' queries—operates on a different terrain and works according to a different idea of philosophical speculation. To begin with, the "on-the-wayness" of Heidegger's work has everything to do with the absence of the spirit of revenge: by accepting his eternal on-the-wayness, Heidegger overcomes the revulsion of the "It was." He is not on the way to get somewhere specific in his essays any more than he wants to be master over his subject. His mastery is the mastery of the novice who always lives in the middle of what he is doing without attempting to overcome the "It was" that always seems to precede the middle where he finds himself. The essential open-endedness of Heidegger's questions and essays shows that he is quite willing to let time pass without revulsion toward its passing. In allowing language to speak him, he has been delivered from the spirit of revenge and is willing to let the openness of his essays stand as it is.

The openness of the questions, however, and the open-endedness of the essays, does not mean that nothing is resolved or that Heidegger is content merely to let time pass while he is on the way to thinking. In being on the way to thinking, he is accomplishing a great deal, for thought can only occur when one is open to respond to the ideas that present themselves along the way. Being on the way means that Heidegger is a full participant in the process of thinking: he has taken up an orientation to his thinking and has agreed to follow it where it will lead him. His orientation has built into it the assumption that openness toward thought is the precondition for thinking, both by making oneself available for thought, as Heidegger would have it, and by giving shape to that openness through the contexts one brings to it. Heidegger's one thought may be the relationship between Being and beings, but that thought embraces everything, including the openness of attitude and the acceptance of being in the middle, a position one must adopt because the desire to bring things to an end is the desire for revenge against the passing of time, and also because man himself is inevitably always in the middle, allowing what is to emerge through language's speaking of him. Heidegger's openness thus accomplishes a great deal even if it does not resolve anything. The openness establishes the essential connection among the aesthetic, the true and the good; it demonstrates the middling nature of man; it establishes an attitude toward thinking; and it provides us with an example of the overcoming of revulsion against time. These are all fundamental accomplishments and well worth attending to in their own right. If Heidegger had done nothing more, his work would have value for us for these reasons alone.

Related to these fundamental insights is Heidegger's conception of the truth of *aletheia*, which is yet another crucial aspect of the lyrical nature of his questions. Our traditions are based on the revelatory nature of truth, but seeing truth in terms of unconcealment is radically different from the pure light of revelation. The word *unconcealment* always has *conceal* built into it in a way that *reveal* does not, and this is important for Heidegger because for him truth always remains attached to the concealment in which it originally exists. Through language it may be brought into the foreground and hence become unconcealed, but its truth value resides in its inherent connection to the background out of which it emerges. Its value is connected to the fact that it was concealed, that it can become concealed again if man chooses to forget it, and that it carries its concealedness with it, for in coming to the fore and announcing itself, it conceals something else in the process, the background out of which it came.

Once again Heidegger takes a stance in direct opposition

to the traditional dictates of reason, for to see truth in terms of unconcealedness is also to see it as essentially context bound. Inasmuch as the goal of reason is to arrive at statements that are true regardless of the context, this notion of truth does not correspond at all to the ideal of reason. Truth can be seen as unconcealedness only so long as one understands it in its relation to the domain out of which it came. This does not mean, of course, that truth is relative; what it does mean is that it reveals a different character in the scene of its emergence than it does considered by itself and equally that the nature of its character is dependent on its manner of emergence from that context.

To conceive of truth in this way may seem bizarre—it even seems to be a negation of the word *truth* altogether to some—but in principle that is not the case. Most generally it is simply a part of Heidegger's concern with our forgetfulness of Being. If it is language that allows beings to emerge into unconcealedness, it is also true that the particular beings that emerge remain connected to Being itself, even if It remains concealed to us in our forgetfulness. In this sense Heidegger is simply trying to redirect our attention away from beings as beings and toward beings in their relationship to Being itself. Man's use of reason has led him to analyze the differences between beings, and at that reason has been quite adept, but in so doing it has led us away from the difference inherent in the Being/being relationship, and that has generated erroneous conceptions about the nature of beings, the most obvious of which is that they are there for us to manipulate for our own purposes in the belief that there are no consequences inherent in these manipulations.

The stumbling blocks to Heidegger's insight here are two. First, as his own repeated remarks about Being suggest, there is ultimately little to be said about it short of pointing to it and explaining in a general way how beings in their unconcealedness are related to the still-concealed Being. As with concepts like "identity" or "ego," the word *Being* is ultimately mysterious, and thus there is the question of how illuminating continual reference to it is. Second, there is the very real question whether *Being* refers to anything at all, or whether its mysteri-

ousness resides precisely in the fact that it covers up an absence rather than a presence, as such writers as Derrida and
Heidegger himself have considered at times. If rather than
"Being" there is really nothing—or at least nothing about
which we can know anything—then what does this do to the
nature of truth as unconcealedness? In part, this is a problem
inherent in the word *Being* itself, for whatever it might be,
there is very little that one can say about it. This is the residue
of the Kantian problem of the thing-in-itself, that fundamentally unknowable category that still lives a phantom existence
today in places. There can be no doubt that for Heidegger the
question of Being was paramount, but ontological questions
have been so thoroughly compromised by the philosophical
inquiries of the past century that for our purposes it is best to
put the issue of Being in abeyance and adopt a more pragmatic
stance toward that which we know of the world.

To refuse to employ a concept of Being is not to deny the
value of truth as unconcealedness, though. In discussing the
nature of the work of art, for example, Heidegger puts the
same problem in a different way:

Truth establishes itself in the work. Truth is present only as the
conflict between lighting and concealing in the opposition of the
world and earth. The conflict is not to be resolved in a being brought
forth for the purpose, nor is it to be merely housed there; the conflict,
on the contrary, is started by it. In the strife the unity of world and
earth is won. As a world opens itself, it submits to the decision of
an historical humanity the question of victory and defeat, blessing
and curse, mastery and slavery. The dawning world brings out what
is as yet undecided and measureless, and thus discloses the hidden
necessity of measure and decisiveness. ["The Origin of the Work of
Art," in *Poetry, Language, Thought,* trans. Albert Hofstadter (New
York: Harper and Row, 1971), pp. 62–63.]

The distinction here between world and earth is not precisely the same as that between Being and beings, yet the
relationship is the same. The world emerges from the earth
through the work of art and maintains an essential relationship to that earth. The relationship is based on the conflict

between world and earth, a conflict introduced by the emergence of beings from the earth into the world. The world of human culture as it emerges from the earth is always based on this conflict, yet it maintains its essential connection to the earth as well. The emergence of the world in this sense is a violence done to the earth, for it ruptures it and sets it in conflict with itself, but at the same time the emergence of the world also allows the earth to emerge into unconcealedness. In paying attention to what happens in the background as the world emerges from the earth, Heidegger focuses our attention on the way earth is changed by the manner through which we allow the world to emerge.

Again, there is the problem of the status of the earth—has it become merely another placeholder for the mysterious word *Being?* Is it as essentially unknowable as the thing-in-itself? Should we instead confine ourselves to speaking about worlds emerging from other worlds and concede that the use of *earth* here is merely another convenient fiction? I would argue to the contrary, for Heidegger makes it clear that the earth is only visible through the conflict with the world, so there is no sense in which it can be construed as the world purified of human vision. The earth too only emerges through the development of the world and always remains concealed and unconcealed because of its strife with it. And this is the case even if it is also true that worlds emerge from earlier worlds as well and thus engage the conflict with the earth through a redefinition of other worlds that have emerged. Why, then, if we are willing to abandon the word *Being* are we unwilling to abandon the word *earth?* Because the world that emerges is the world of human history and human choices, and those choices produce effects. Heidegger tells us that "the dawning world brings out what is yet undecided and measureless," but it is also the world through which the decisions and the measure of the earth will be gauged. We may only know of the earth through the measures and decisions we inaugurate in the world we allow to emerge, but those choices are tested through their effects on the earth and the earth's effects on them. The world and the earth are always in conflict because the measure of the world is not totally consonant with the measure of the earth, and the result is that in some cases the measure of the world extends and develops the measure of the earth and in others the earth corrects the measure of the world. The conflict between the two is thus also a connection, for the measures of each do correspond in places and reinforce each other. In so doing, the measure of the earth confirms the measure of the world, and the measure of the world brings into unconcealment aspects of the earth that were previously hidden.

At a more specific level, the principle of truth as unconcealment is in its own way akin to the science of ecology, which likewise recognizes the effects of the world on the earth—though its attention is less directed to the effects of the earth on the world—and is devoted to discerning how human measure intrudes upon and affects the earth. It is based on the premise that local changes have larger effects, that the decisions made in the foreground of a context also affect the background, and it is equally based on the relation of the background context to the foreground that emerges. One cannot conceive of the effluents from a single factory in isolation, for to do so is to ignore how they affect other activities in the area and the larger cycles of which those activities are equally a part. One must consider the relationship between the local choice and the fields of which it is a part rather than one or the other in isolation.

At the same time, only man's repeated choices in ignorance of this relationship have forced us to alter our measure to suit the earth. Only when our world was developed sufficiently enough to show how the series of choices it led to worked against the measure of the earth were we once again properly able to conceive of the conflict and connection that exists between world and earth. The growth of our world, if you will, arrived at the point where it became clear in all too many ways that the world's measure conflicted with the earth's in thoroughly incompatible ways. Heidegger's conception of unconcealedness is no more than one of the many changes in the world's measure—from the theory of relativity to the establishment of ecology—that were available to man because there was an essential conflict between world and earth and because it was visible everywhere.

When Heidegger urges upon us the conception of truth as unconcealedness, he is not merely being quixotic, for truth as unconcealedness is intimately bound up once again with man's revulsion against time. To conceive of truth as unconcealedness, to admit that something is concealed in every unconcealment, is once again to submit ourselves to the "It was" and to overcome the desire for revenge that is at the heart of truth as revelation. It is no more of an accident that reason, science, and technology developed out of the same revulsion against time that further encouraged the spirit of revenge than it is an accident that the spirit of revenge and the revulsion against time become clearly visible only when truth as unconcealment emerges from the conflict with truth as revelation. Truth as unconcealment begins with the premise that there can be no truth as revelation, that the truth of revelation is devoted to a negation of time that is not possible and is based finally on the desire for revenge.

At this point, Heidegger's work begins to raise questions of the kind Nietzsche himself fought with, particularly in the idea of the eternal return. If it is the case that truth is unconcealedness, the question is whether or not mankind can bear that thought, and secondarily, if he can indeed bear it, can he allow a world to emerge on the basis of it? The thought itself is difficult to bear both because of the complexities it introduces and because of the perspective and attitude it requires of man. We are forced to see ourselves as less powerful than we thought we were and must recognize that our power derives from our acceptance of our less-powerful position. Even more, we must also be able to turn away from our revulsion against time and thus against our desire for revenge. Nietzsche was quite right in calling this the bridge to the overman simply because man has been resisting such impulses for millennia. Taken as we are with our own sense of power—and equally driven by our perpetual sense of weakness—we have repeatedly argued that it resides in the strength of our desire for revenge and our hopes to negate time, and to abjure the enticement of this view is perhaps more than we are capable of. And if we are to believe Freud when he tells us that the pleasure principle and the death instinct are ultimately inseparable, how could we possibly hope to be delivered from revenge, the most obvious facet of the death instinct? We would have to be more than human to do so. At the very least, one would have to concede that it is no simple matter to have done with our incessant desire for revenge.

As for the complexity of choices that results from truth as unconcealment and the openness it requires, how could we possibly attend to them and still act regularly in the world? How could we begin to develop a system of values that would at once be based on truth as unconcealment and also be suitable for everyday life? These are the kinds of questions and burdens for man that the work of Nietzsche and Heidegger raise, and there are no simple answers to them. In reconnecting the aesthetic to the true, and in accepting their essential relationship to the good, Heidegger and Nietzsche have left us on a seemingly open terrain without direction, but that is not really the case. The pathway they have opened up with their lyrical questions is certainly somewhat unfamiliar to us, and yet its resemblance to the way we do things as a matter of course is rather uncanny. Our daily actions defy the dictates of reason all the time, and we feel no great discomfort in that as a rule. Likewise, our action in the world is often based on the kind of openness we see at work in Heidegger and Nietzsche. Perhaps, then, if we begin to see how much of our activity actually corresponds to the ideas Nietzsche and Heidegger illuminate, we might be able to trace the consequences of our revulsion against time and our desire for revenge in a way that will allow us to be delivered from their sway and to live more comfortably under the reign of the lyrical.

2 Discursivity and Recursivity

We have lived until recently in a discursive world, and our questions have led us there. Our questions, however, discursive as they have been, have always finally led us back to a principle of recursivity as well. We hammered as best we could at the older, circular vision of time in an attempt to transform it into a line as straight as an arrow, but the tip of the arrow only increased our revulsion against time, and as our revulsion increased, we began to see the circles of time that escaped our line. We laid out a similar line of reason and connected it to progress, but the line would not remain straight, curved back upon itself, and began to generate once again the cycle of the ages. The limit of the line grew to be too much, however hard we tried to believe in it, and the result was that we began to feel as though we had reached the end of it. Indeed, we seemed to reach the limits of the line just about everywhere at the same time: reason was called into question, imperialism began to run into insuperable obstacles, Newtonian space turned out to be too flat and static, and Euclid needed to be improved upon while developments of a similar kind in most other Western domains continued to appear. The discursive world had reached its limits, and recursivity reasserted itself with ever stronger force, regularly to be resisted.

One could argue, with McLuhan and others, that the emphasis on discursivity was related to the changes in discourse brought about by the introduction of the printing press and that the reemergence of the recursive has to do with the obsolescence of print as a medium. There are no doubt some correlations here, but it is equally true that the printing press was preceded by discursive tendencies in thought just as the recursive reappeared long before there were media to complement it. Whereas the technology clearly helped to spread tendencies of thought, it seems more likely that the technology emerged from the questions that were asked and, in recursive fashion, reinforced the strength of those questions. But there is no doubt that a discursive view of the world began to emerge in the Renaissance and only began to turn back on itself about one hundred years ago—someone like Nietzsche is a clear mark of that turning.

If the linear view of existence was so powerful over the past few centuries, there must have been good reasons for its strength inasmuch as a world only emerges in consort with the historical humans who give it life and support. In part, the discursive view of the world was appealing because it seemed to lead man out of the desire for revenge and the revulsion against time. The most basic of vicious circles is constituted by reciprocal revenge extending itself infinitely, and linearity suggests a breaking of that circle, reinforced by the idea of progress that complements the time line. Progress may appear as the desire to transform the earth through technological change, but it can only be taken seriously when it offers the possibility of escaping the circular revulsion against time, and discursivity seems to do that, at least for a while. A time line extending into the future grants man a greater degree of control over what is to come—at least up to the end of the line—and it seems to leave the repetitions and reoccurrences of revenge behind in the process.

Seen in this light, discursivity is the opportunity to transcend time and so escape revulsion of it. Sequentiality assures that one thing comes after another without repetition, and in one sense it is the ultimate ritual for avoiding the demons of man. We took sequentiality as the perfect method for ordering our lives, obsessively laying down the parameters of the world in serial terms in order to assure that they did not recur, to keep them from coming back to haunt us. Discursivity and reason became the ultimate magic against the demons of revenge, and the monoplanar view of the world that we developed from them allowed everything to have its own place without the worry that dangerous chemicals might combine, erupt, and return man to the vicious circles he was

seeking to escape. As the flat earth became round, we transformed a round world into a flat one, and up through much
of the nineteenth century it almost seemed like our magic
worked.

The problem was that it was magic, and man was no magician. The virtue of the discursive model was that it invented
man, but man assumed erroneously that he had control, when
in fact the invention had a life of its own. An essential aspect
of the linear world was that man controlled it, so it was not
written into the script that he would see himself responding
to changes he in part helped to initiate. Rather, the world was
stable and waited inertly for man to work his magic upon it
without affecting the spell or turning it against humans. In
this sense, books like Mary Shelley's *Frankenstein* do not suggest that science will come back to haunt man; rather, they
reassert the recursive principle inherent in all systems: the
world as it emerges affects man as well, but from a discursive
viewpoint, he only begins to see those effects when the world
seems to take on a life of its own. The revulsion against the
monster we have created is misplaced only because it is not
simply a monster we have created: it is a revulsion against
time and its "It was," which we thought we had left comfortably behind us, but which returned instead as a mutation of
the world we allowed to emerge. The monster is thus our
own desire for revenge come back to haunt us once again,
and the revenge of the monster is the result of our revulsion
against him. The world that was to take us away from time
could not do so because a large part of our investment in life
was saturated with our revulsion. The contempt displaced
within the discursive model toward the earth guaranteed that
it would feel our revulsion and reciprocate with its own.
Linearity thus became not an escape from the revulsion we
felt but rather led to an exacerbation of it. The earth absorbed
our poisonous magic, but we were also nourished by the
earth, so we reingested the poison in more concentrated quan-
tities.

The fear of recursivity, the fear of the return, the fear of
reciprocation, and the fear of replication are all at the center of
our desire for a discursive world, and rather than overcoming

them, we only displaced them. It was then up to Freud to invent a new location for these fears and to tell us how they got there, why they were always displaced, and what the consequences of the displacements were. The great virtue of Freud's work was not only that it showed how we never left these fears behind, or our lack of control over them; it was also that it located the fears squarely within us. We could no longer look elsewhere for the origin of the terrors that dominated our lives. They were not outside, to be controlled by our linear analyses; they were inside, directing the very linearity that was supposed to eliminate their effectiveness. Three hundred years of discursivity led us back to that which we were seeking to avoid, the fear of the return, the revulsion against time. Freud undermined our sense of control by describing what had control over us and, by showing us that we had not escaped what we thought we had, our own sense of revulsion. We devoted ourselves to the grand attempt to transcend time, and when we had to confront our revulsion openly once again, our distress was acute.

The fear of return was even more obvious in Freud because he also provided an origin for it, the primal murder of the father that we all seek to keep from recurring. Even if the primal murder was nothing more than a metaphor for our hidden desires, it brought back our fear of recurrence and showed us why we fear the return. Reciprocal violence and the fear of replication—our return with a difference—are the locus of our revulsion against time, for the primal murder is part of the irretrievable "It was" about which we can do nothing, and the fear of reciprocation and replication is the repetition of the "It was" within ourselves. This is why the notion of individualism and its connection to linearity are so strong: by conferring godlike, autonomous powers on each individual, and by granting each individual his own definite time line, we have protected him from the incursions of recurrence, of reciprocation, of replication. But the notions of autonomy that go along with individualism cannot keep their purity, much as we try to maintain them, and the result is that the self becomes more fragile as it seeks to protect itself on the slender thread of autonomy. In turn, it comes to feel a greater revulsion against time, for if our desire to avoid replication is tied to our revulsion, our replication as members of the human species allows us in some sense to escape the disgust we feel toward our past by generating a future. The autonomous self is incapable of seeing its progeny—be they children or the results of its work—as being healthy replication, the necessary recursivity that allows man to overcome his revulsion against the past. Thus, the autonomous self, an apparently ideal solution to our problems, ends up becoming not only sterile but also deadly.

In this light, we get a stronger sense of why Nietzsche and Heidegger are so threatening to us. After all, in one way or another they are often accused of attempting to destroy that great edifice we call Western civilization. The arguments for such a proposition would point to their denial of the efficacy of reason or to their irrationality. But these reasons do not fully account for the extreme hostility both thinkers have been exposed to—they are rather the displaced arguments of those who fear the return of the return, of recursivity. Given such fears, it is far better to characterize the one as a madman and the other as a quasi-mystical, otherworldly type who also dabbled in fascism. This tames their ideas, for who would want to be associated with such characters? Equally apparent, such ploys demonstrate most accurately where these fears come from, for they reflect a dread of infection and warn us against it by showing us what we will become if we think seriously about them. In fearing the return of replication and repetition, we lay blame for the repetition on them; after all, they are the ones who let the genie out of the bottle again. And if Western societies are to remain strong, they must keep their genies bottled up; they must repress the fear of return, for to concede its existence is to undermine the world that was designed to eliminate it.

If, however, we are to accept the return of the return, what is to compensate us for conceding the existence of the vicious circle of revenge and our revulsion against time? If recursivity does exist and does manifest itself within this vicious circle, are not we perhaps better off leaving it hidden, particularly inasmuch as our fears of it clearly demonstrate our knowledge of its power? Should we not simply concede that this is one area that discursivity is incapable of dealing with and continue to act as though it does not exist? In this we would be doing no more than following a great tradition, for man's attempts to ignore these fears began long before discursivity became the operative principle of our world. One is reminded of the scene early in *Oedipus Rex* where Oedipus, attempting to discern the origin of the plague, asks the people if they ever found Laius' killer. Their response is that other things like the Sphinx occupied their minds, and anyway, "Out of sight was out of mind." They knew better than to probe too far; when the plague goes away, one ought to have the sense to refuse to seek its origin. And certainly Oedipus himself is our primal reminder of this: the knowledge of the origin of the plague is not what we think it is, and it will even undo us. Out of sight is out of mind.

Nietzsche and Heidegger are acutely aware of the vicious circle, however, and unlike some of their successors, they treat the problem with the care that it requires. In addition to arguing that we must finally come to deal with man's revulsion against time, though, they are not simply dealing with the negative aspects of human nature. On the contrary, they confront the evil of the return only because of the good of the return; they choose to deal with the vicious cycle of reciprocation only because they must in order to deal with the virtuous cycle of reciprocation, what Heidegger would call the hermeneutic circle of understanding. If the vicious circle of revenge is destructive, the circle of understanding is productive—if one destroys in its attempt to avoid reproducing, the other increases life through its replication. The rhapsodic strains of the poet always bear an uncanny resemblance to the equally ecstatic outbursts of the violent madman. Recursivity, the regular return with a difference, is the inherent principle in all understanding—the difference in the return is always that which is understood, and it is always that which increases our understanding of the whole through which the difference returns. The same is true for all of the other moments of life based on the reciprocation of the good—the differences displayed in a conversation or any other meaningful relationship provide understanding of the same, and in becoming unconcealed, the differences highlight not only the differences but also the same, allowing one or the other to be focused on in accord with the lines of interest. Here the principle of difference manifests itself in a positive light, so long as it is also connected to the same, and the differences demonstrate why the truth must both conceal and unconceal at the same time—even more, the differences demonstrate why understanding is only possible if both the concealed and the unconcealed are seen in their essential relationship together. For if we have a fear of replication, we also have a fear of difference, and when we are not concerned about our own reproduction in another location, we are concerned that we are *not* being reproduced. If we fear the reciprocal return of the same and its displacement of us, we equally fear the lack of reciprocal return of us with a difference. We do not wish to return as the same, yet we do not wish to return with a difference. The hermeneutic circle is thus based on the necessity of keeping both the return of the same and the return of difference in view—the circle needs to maintain this dialectic in order to preserve the differencing of difference and the difference of the same; if that cannot be done, the hermeneutic circle turns into the vicious circle, and the ecstasy of understanding turns into the ecstasy of destruction and fear.

How then are we to deal with the fear of difference and the fear of the same? We could, like Freud, begin to understand them in terms of the life instinct (connected to the libido) and the death instinct (connected to the ego). The fear of difference would be seen as a manifestation of the ego's death instinct, its desire to return to an earlier, more simplified, basically inorganic state. The repetition compulsion is as a result an attempt to master difference by eliminating it, by restricting the world to the repetition of the same, which is equally an attempt to negate time and its "It was." The revulsion against difference is both a bid to preserve the purity of the ego and an attempt to annihilate it in all its purity. Any difference would be seen as an intrusion of time on the ego and thus a corrupting influence on that which desires to be preserved. The repetitions attempt to negate both past and future in order to eliminate the ego's connection to time—the death instinct only seems to be a desire for immortality in this context; rather, it is the desire for death that is at the heart of the fear of difference.

The life instinct would in turn be the desire to overcome the sameness of repetition, the desire not only to embrace but to disseminate difference as well, to perpetuate the growth of the world through the generation of further difference. It does not so much fear the same as desire to negate it through the spread of difference, which, as in the sex act itself, is always a recursive process, involving the return of the same with a difference—the genes are mixed, but they do reappear. The life instinct does not fear the same then; it denies its existence altogether by connecting it irretrievably to difference. This in turn means that the fear of the same, like the fear of difference, is embodied in the death instinct rather than the life instinct, that the repetition compulsion not only manifests the fear of difference but also the fear of the same. The repetition of the same creates the sense of having eliminated difference, but, as in narcissistic cases, it therefore leaves one within the vicious circle of the same—it is an essentially masturbatory act that ultimately leaves one in boredom, the revulsion against the same. The vicious circle of revenge is thus bound on the one side by the revulsion against difference, time, and the "It was," but it is also bound by the revulsion against the same, stasis, and death.

Nietzsche's thought of the eternal return is the complement to being delivered from revenge, for the ego—devoted to the death instinct in order to eliminate difference—is equally repulsed by the consequence of such repetitions—the return of the same—so that the acceptance of the eternal return of the same is likewise a way of breaking out of the egocentric desire to escape that which one has created, the return of the same. To concede the return is to accept the one's desire for it, which is based on the r difference, and this allows the vicious circle t for difference to return. Only the subordinati the life instinct allows the vicious circle to be

If, however, one concedes that the fear of

the fear of the same are both connected to the death instinct, would it not be more appropriate to argue for the elimination of the death instinct altogether? Would not that more thoroughly resolve the problem than merely subordinating it to the life instinct? In one sense this is probably true, for the only way to eliminate the fear of difference would be to deny the death instinct altogether. To do so, though, would mean the elimination of the instinct and the ego, and whereas this might rid us of the fear of difference, it would also destroy one of the crucial differences in the world, which is the ego itself. Even more, the death instinct is unavoidably connected to the life instinct—it dialectically forces the life instinct to generate further difference; it is precisely the life instinct's fight against the sameness of death that prompts it further to disseminate difference against death. Within the human, too, the awareness of repetition pushes one to new differences; the movement away from the same we have attempted to repeat leads to difference just as the attempt to return to the same leads to difference. Inasmuch as this is the case, one cannot ultimately separate the life instinct from the death instinct, as reason tries to do; one can only assure the predominance of the life instinct by granting its essential connection to the death instinct.

We have not really moved away from a fear of difference or a fear of the same, then, for neither can be eliminated without destroying the dialectic that makes up life. We can only reorient ourselves to the dialectic by placing ourselves under its sway, by agreeing to participate within it and by refusing to be revolted by the play of time in which it involves us. Only the difference between the two allows difference to emerge, and only by placing ourselves within the circle of that difference can we hope to escape our desire for vengeance.

The difference between discursive and recursive views of the world is that the discursive view attempts to escape the circle of revenge by denying its existence, by turning the world into a monoplanar structure devoid of circularity, just as within the narrower compass of reason the law of noncontradiction and the negation of circular arguments are the keynes to the preservation of the analytic method. The recur-

sive view denies the value of the law of noncontradiction—
except for a circumscribed area of usefulness—and asserts
that all arguments, and all questions, are fundamentally circular. To accept circularity is to accede to the return of the same,
but the denial of the law of noncontradiction assures that the
circles will never be the same, that they will always return
with a difference. Methodologically speaking, this fully accounts for Heidegger's regular insistence that all great thinkers have only one idea—in his case the relationship of beings
to Being—while at the same time that one idea regularly
appears differently. If Heidegger always only asks about the
relationship of beings to Being—or perhaps more fundamentally why there is something rather than nothing—yet the
same question, as it returns to the terrain of Heidegger's
earlier attempts to answer the question, always returns with
a difference. Something new is always brought to light because the context has changed and because the way of asking
the question is informed by the difference in context. This is
equally why Heidegger felt no need to disguise the fact that
he was always asking the same question; he assumed from
the outset that he could do nothing other than ask the same
question and was confident that his way of asking it would
always generate something different. A recursive question
always returns with a difference because it accepts from the
outset that difference itself is that which allows questions to
emerge to begin with and thus assures their difference.

It is easy enough to see how the discursive view is designed
to eliminate the return of the same by denying any role to
circular reasoning, but the value of the law of noncontradiction in this context is less clear. And inasmuch as within the
realm of reason the law of noncontradiction is conceived of
as the very cornerstone of thought, we need to ask why it is
so essential and why the recursive view must ultimately deny
its force. If the law of noncontradiction states that one cannot
say both that something is and is not the case, how does that
allow our logic to proceed? Why is that an essential first
assumption to make? One could say that this move assures a
certain consistency of thought, for it denies one the right to
argue two cases at the same time, and that seems reasonable

enough, even if it does reduce the stream of thought to a two-dimensional surface. The kind of consistency that requires a two-dimensional beginning, middle, and end is clearly dependent upon one not arguing two things at the same time. Only poets are allowed to contradict themselves, and that is because no one pays any attention to them anyway. More fundamentally, though, the law of noncontradiction assures that any argument will not return upon itself; it assures that the line will only go forward without return. The law of noncontradiction is based on keeping differences different so they do not return as the same. It insists that everything exists in its own discrete space and its own discrete time, and that it is only by keeping everything distinct that one can arrive at the end of a line of reasoning. The law of noncontradiction assures that the chain of differences can only be arranged in one way, so it asserts the essentiality of difference in order to assume the return of the same—only by keeping the differences discrete can we hope to arrive at a reproducible response that guarantees the sameness of the result. The law of noncontradiction is thus designed to remove thought from the dialectic of discourse and turn it into the straight line of infinite reproducibility. In that context, it should be clear how the age of reason could so easily transform itself into the age of information, for information is the logical end point of this linear process: one is left with an infinite amount of reproducible data that seems to confirm the value of the linear process that generated it, so long as one does not worry about what to do with all the information one has obtained. To extend the argument to a familiar context these days, one could say that the discursive mode was designed to take thought out of the range of speech and put it into the domain of print, with the assumption that print guaranteed the non-circularity of thought because it moves in only one direction. This in turn led to Nietzsche and Heidegger, who reasserted the dialectic of speech over the linearity of writing, which in turn led to Derrida, who denied the power of speech to take precedence over writing at the same time that he denied the power of writing to avoid the dialectic of speech. For Derrida, the problem with the logic of a thinker like Husserl was that it proceeded on the lines of writing but was really only a disguised assertion of the pure priority of speech: in order to assure the purity of the line of reasoning, it had to be based on a moment of pure presence, a moment *before* difference had asserted itself. For Derrida this is the contradiction inherent in all logical thought, and it leads him to deny the existence of the voice altogether. For our purposes the distinction between speech and writing does not make that much difference, for the voice of Heidegger begins with difference in any case and so is not dependent on an initial moment of purity—the initial, original utterance does not exist for Heidegger, so speech and writing are both founded on difference.

By way of example, though, one could say that the discursive practices of writing seek to overcome the dialectic of conversation, of speech, for the conversation always requires the difference of at least two voices, even if both of them are one's own. It presupposes that conversation only proceeds by the return of difference, as one line of thought turns into its opposite, as the differences of one line head inevitably to the assertion of another line. Just as in a conversation one ultimately ends up holding more than one proposition, just as the one proposition is dependent on its difference from another, so too in recursive thought it is assumed that the law of noncontradiction exists only to be violated. And once the logic of the conversation makes this clear, contradiction—essential difference—cannot be overcome because it is there from the beginning. The discursive world seeks to iron out the wrinkles of conversation, if you will, so that a satisfactory conclusion can be reached. The discursive question is based on the premise that one's query always reaches a conclusion that in turn allows one to build further questions on the conclusions of previous ones. The recursive question, in contrast, assumes from the outset that the lines of difference that generated the question to begin with make it inevitable that no single resolution can be arrived at, that, on the contrary, it is the play of differences within the question that leads to movement rather than the resolution of the question itself. Socrates' conversations fail to reach a particular resolution not because they *cannot* arrive at one but because Socrates does not see that form of resolution as part of questioning to begin with. For him the conversation inevitably turns back on itself many times, gathering new force as it does so, but not with the goal of a particular resolution in mind. Likewise, Heidegger does not see the conclusions of his essays as an end of the conversation but rather as a return to the beginning of the discussion with a difference—one is again ready to take up the question at the end, but with the understanding gained by having already taken it up.

The practical ends of discursivity and recursivity are thus quite different. The goal of discursivity is to be able to put what one has learned to use, and the same is true for the recursive, but use is defined differently. For the discursive, use is defined in terms of an instrument through which to manipulate things; for the recursive, it is defined in terms of an instrument through which to measure things. The one seeks to make use of things outside of the context in which they are originally found; the other seeks to make use of things through and in the context in which they are located. The recursive uses the question to open up the terrain of the context of the query while the discursive employs the question to transcend the context of it. Inasmuch as the discursive question must always be reintroduced into a context to have any value, however, it ultimately has to accept the premises of recursivity anyway. It seeks to escape recursive logic by breaking the process into discrete steps, but ultimately the steps become part of the same circle they were designed to escape.

If the discursive always capitulates to the recursive, then, what is its value to begin with? If we come to see that any particular discursive practice ultimately feeds back into a larger recursive activity, what is the value of trying to keep the two discrete? From a purely discursive view, the value is that one can try to escape the power of the recursive by sticking to the linearity of the line, but if each such line always becomes a part of the larger recursivity in any case, this value is only an illusion that blinds one to the processes of which one is really a part. If, however, one makes use of the discursive in the knowledge that it is part of recursiveness and inseparable from it, it allows one to trace the consequences of various lines of discourse and to demonstrate the ways in which they recur with a difference in various domains. The practical effect of this attitude is that it allows the discursive a greater power by showing how its power is connected to a recursive range of dissemination across various discursive practices. It turns the various discourses into a series of cross-fertilizing enterprises instead of a series of discontinuous time lines stretching infinitely into the distance without touching. The power of the discursive resides in its dissemination across lines of discourse rather than in the preservation of an illusory purity of discourse, but that can only be seen when the essential connection to the recursive is admitted. And likewise, something which Heidegger himself did not attend to as much as he should have, the recursive gains its power only from its connection to the discursive, only from its connection to the lines of thought that make any return possible to begin with. It is the discursive that allows the recursive to be always a return with a difference; it ultimately keeps the circle of understanding from becoming a vicious circle of revenge.

To repudiate the law of noncontradiction and to accept the circularity of discourse is thus not to deny the law of noncontradiction its function—it is only to put it in its place, subordinate to the recursivity it seeks to dominate but cannot. The larger question inherent in this argument is still the question of difference: if we live at a time when the power of difference has been asserted over the force of the same, how did we arrive at this moment? If it is the power of the same that has driven thought in the West for so long, why does it now return to be subordinated to difference? Most generally, it is clear that the recursive began to appear as the limits of the power of the discursive began to be reached, and this seemed to occur in most domains at a similar moment. It was not just that Euclidean geometry failed to account sufficiently for the data of the world, that Newtonian theory failed to account for similar phenomena, that Western imperialism began to be changed by the peoples it sought to dominate, that man's sense of himself and his godlike powers began to be seriously questioned at the same time God himself was

called into question. These shifts themselves were the result
of discursive practice and the contradictions inherent in it. It
assumed that there was no limit to its practice (something
that ran counter to its desire for a negation of time) and
asserted the presence of an independent eye that supposedly
directed discursive practice—an eye that was seen increasingly to be focusing on its own twitches rather than revealing
the reality independent of its gaze. Its own investigations
thus culminated in the simple historical necessity of accepting
that while discursive practice was instrumental in changing
the features of the world and the metaphors through which
it was defined, the basic data of human life and history resisted its attempts at change and instead caused the discursive
increasingly to confront that which it most sought to ignore:
man's revulsion against time, man's death instinct at the center of the linear view of the world. A Nietzsche or a Freud
does not appear as an idiosyncratic outburst that is irrelevant
to the discourse as a whole: he appears as a manifestation of
that which the system can no longer ignore.

   The initial limit of power in the discursive system is marked
by the bits of existence that do not fit into the practice, but
gradually they come to be seen as a failure of transcendence.
The eye of science fails to escape man's limit and offers no
prospect of doing so; the "I" of Romantic transcendence leads
not to a new world but rather increasingly makes the old one
look more desperate; the high abstractions of philosophical
speculation come to be seen as antagonistic to the reality they
are said to interpret; the colonialism begins to corrupt as much
as it civilizes. In each case, the transcendent possibility begins
to diminish, and with that possibility goes the power to transform the earth according to our own specifications. In turn,
ideas such as Freud's emerge when the double life of humans
begins to become apparent, when discursive practice must
begin to deal with the fact that it has failed to tame the world,
even failed to account for that which needed to be tamed. In
this regard the modern era was no different from previous
ones, for it sought to locate that which needed to be tamed
outside of man—the difference was that it committed its entire
apparatus of knowledge to tracking down the beast in the

jungle and argued that only its knowledge would tame it. When it did finally track down the beast, its apparatus could only leave it to conclude that the problem was not "out there" but rather inside of the man who had developed the means to contain it. Even at that Freud's work not only locates the origin of the problem within man but also seeks to tame it through discursive practice, the talking cure that civilizes. Freud was simply an imperialist of the mind rather than of other cultures.

It is a double life, though, that ultimately makes it impossible for man to ignore the limits of discursivity, for once he acknowledges the double life he also has to concede that the discursive cannot adequately account for the other man—it banished him with the law of non-contradiction, and that he should return is the final refutation of the ultimate powers of the discursive. The doubles manifest themselves not only in the conscious/unconscious duality, though they are most pervasively obvious in that couplet; they equally appear through the double lives people see themselves leading and in diseases such as schizophrenia. The schizophrenic may be the limit of the double life, but that which he marks is found in everyone devoted to the law of reason: the narrow realm of existence enframed by the logical and consistent, and the rest of man bounded by an altogether different system of action and motivation. If there were an ultimate value to the practice of reason, it would be that it made it extremely difficult for man to ignore his double life and thus forced him to confront it, running counter to reason yet stemming from the consequences of its pathways. The law of noncontradiction was established to eliminate the death instinct, but its glory was to lead finally to the point where man had to face it.

I should emphasize once again, however, that the limits of discursivity do not lead to its negation; rather, they simply place it where it belongs, within the recursive flows of discourse and thought. The recursive may always be on the way to something and may accept the end as ironic, but it must also see the discursivity within its returns if it is to avoid slipping into the abyss and into mere flux. To return to Derrida, the "joyous affirmation" is never enough, for the return of the aesthetic alone fails to account for the choices made *within* the joyous affirmation. One cannot joyously affirm in a vacuum; one always does so through a particular context, and the values of the chosen scene always become an essential part of the affirmation. Derrida tacitly agrees to this by accepting that his deconstructive operations always involve him in the ontotheological system he seeks to lay bare; his values in this sense are chosen on the basis of which texts he chooses to pursue. His affirmation always takes place in the context of a Hegel or Husserl or Nietzsche, and in doing so his values are revealed. Whereas Derrida would accuse Heidegger of being nostalgic, of trying to get back to the origin of Being before man intruded himself—a partially accurate account— Derrida is also nostalgic, necessarily so with his view of the trace and of deconstruction. And perhaps his nostalgia is even sadder than any Heidegger might have had, for he does not believe in that about which he is nostalgic. In denying or ignoring the fact that there is an earth off of which and into which the world plays, Derrida has left himself always with the backward glance, the reverse orientation, and even if something new is generated out of the deconstruction, one cannot disguise the fact that the orientation leads to a future that is really always only a past.

While Derrida has "civilized" instincts, in other words, his joyous affirmation is not involved necessarily in the deliverance from revenge; clearly, the endlessness of difference and the willingness to play infinitely suggest a movement against the revulsion of time, yet the very endlessness of the backward marking of traces seems to embody within it the seeds of revulsion. Derrida accepts the "It was" of the past, but his acceptance does not lead to the "It was" of the future—the future is always the past, always a different trace but the same line. The entire process of deconstruction is an acceptance of the past that denies the difference of the present or the future: the future is announced, to be sure, but it never appears because in all of the dissemination of difference—or rather in spite of all the dissemination of difference—Derrida's system is finally a closed one; the seed is always spilled but never fertilized. And in this sense what Derrida argues is rather akin to Freud's characterization of the death instinct itself: if not a return to the inorganic, then at least a return to that unicellular domain in which one reproduces oneself infinitely rather than mixing one's genes. On the surface, it is always a play of difference—Hegel against Genet, or whatever—but underneath it is the single cell reproducing itself in the hope that that is enough.

Recursive forms do have their genetic material reproduced in a number of different series, and the system is certainly redundant in that respect, but only to assure the greater likelihood that its code will be picked up and transformed according to the location in which it finds itself. The information is reproduced in each cell, but each cell reproduces the information in a different way and with different results. And it is the discursive within the material that effects the changes in context and leads to different uses of the recursivity. This is why, for example, Heidegger does not find science or technology anathema, as some have charged, for he realizes that the effects of science and technology per se are dependent on the context in which they are embedded, and it is that to which he objects. Seen from within the recursive system of Heidegger, the discursive practices of science and technology are instrumental in transforming the earth into the world in which we live. And whereas part of their initial power stemmed from the idea that they were unconnected to the recursive, this is not an essential aspect of their practice. If they allowed the illusion of pure discourse to flourish, they also helped to bring it to an end and can have even more value for us now that we see how their questions fit into the world that has emerged with them.

The recursive question is always a question of value, of values, not only because it is embedded in particular contexts but also because it is the kind of question to which we always return. The return itself suggests the value of the question for us, and inasmuch as these returns are more often than not unexpected and even unavoidable, we can see such queries as the locus of value. Heidegger, for example, might have devoted himself to the question "Why is there something rather than nothing?" or "What is the relationship between

Being and beings?" and we can see readily enough how those are questions of value. To ask why there is something rather than nothing is first of all to question the value of something-ness over nothingness, but, equally important, it is to question the value of that which is and to try to account for it. In doing so, Heidegger brings out the value of what is and also the values inherent in his relationship to what is, for his questions unfold that which is valuable to him as well as bringing to light the value of the world. Likewise, to ask about the relationship between Being and beings is to bring into focus the basic values of the West, first in assuming that there is such a thing as Being, second in suggesting how Western man has thought of Being—and what that thinking says about the values that he brings to the question—and third in asserting the fundamental value of difference itself by beginning with it. All of these values are in turn transformed into more particular expressions of value on the basis of that which is investigated in terms of the initial question, whether it be the value of thinking, of thingness, of the aesthetic, or whatever. At every level, down to the examples that are used to probe these questions, what is valuable emerges, and it is not only what Heidegger thinks of as valuable that comes to light, for his own questions are obviously dependent on what those before him have conceived of as worthwhile. The return again and again to certain questions, ideas, and thinkers reinforces their value while extending it by the change of context. Just as a literary critic seeks out recurring imagery in a poet's work in an attempt to locate the poet's values, so too can one describe the values inherent in any recursive series of questions.

If such recursivity were only present in a poet's or philosopher's work, it would be interesting enough in its own right, but of course the value of these questions in a poet or a philosopher is present to begin with because our own values are involved in the same questions. It is not likely that the average person spends a great deal of his time asking himself why there is something rather than nothing, or what the relationship of Being to beings is, and yet in particular ways he confronts those questions over and over again throughout his life. It is perhaps true that one only consciously considers such questions during exceptional moments in one's life, but they recur on the everyday level as well. Often the question of why there is something rather than nothing occurs when a context leads one to a desire for negation—when one wishes there were nothing rather than something, either because of an obstacle that one cannot seem to overcome or because of boredom and its accompanying desire to negate time. Often those moments in which we are most pleasingly engaged in living lead us to wonder about why this sense of fullness is not always present. Both of these questions are variants of Heidegger's, and contextually they occur repeatedly and allow us to develop a sense of rightness about our world that fully reveals our values. The virtue of Heidegger's work here is that he has raised these questions in their most salient form, and he has also showed us how to ask them, in particular by accepting from the outset that value is not generated by a single answer to the question but by the recurring way in which the question is asked. Instead of expecting an answer at the end of the questioning that will provide us with a quotient of value, Heidegger shows us how the value is worked out in the questioning, and how the wrong value is attached to the question when we expect it to end in an answer. Discursive as we are, we manifest dissatisfaction when answers are not forthcoming, and Heidegger shows us the value of not expecting an answer. If we are accustomed to feeling that nothing is gained when nothing is specifically answered, Heidegger forces us to ask ourselves what value there is in questions that can be so answered, equally calling into question our sense of what is to be gained from life. The final value of Heidegger's questions turns on the overall sense of worth we give to our lives and the reasons why we ascribe the values to them we do, most specifically when it comes to the value of the projects we frame for ourselves that emanate from the questions we ask and expect ready answers to. We are asked to turn our questions around in order to see what they reveal about us, and then to ask if we really value the "us" we see behind the questions, our way of asking them, and our expectations about answers and values in general.

The recursive question also places the question above the questioner, and this further reveals the sense of value in the query. For Heidegger, man does not so much ask questions as he provides a location for them to arise, and this reverses our normal conception of things. In one sense, the direction of the question for Heidegger goes back as far as *Being and Time* where he characterizes one of the central aspects of human life in terms of "thrownness." Our lives do bear this sense of thrownness—we always arrive too late to know anything about our arrival; our awareness of our existence and its consequences always occurs too late for us ever to be able to locate an origin of anything about us—we cannot trace our steps back to the beginning in order to get a fresh start, nor can we begin to get a sure sense of what led up to our awareness of being here. The questions begin to arise before we can have any hope of knowing where they came from or why any particular set of questions presents itself to us rather than another. Likewise, just as our own history always begins too soon, so too does the history of man always precede us, and the history of its history is so clouded that the origins are hopelessly lost. Given our sense of thrownness, we can adopt the traditional viewpoint and maintain that *we* ask the questions, but this commits us to frame our recursive queries genetically—they must always be devoted to the origin of the questions, for otherwise our investigation will have no ground. And groundless questions undercut the power of the man who raises them: he needs a base, a starting point, in order to assure the power and direction of his inquiries, and without that ground, he can never be sure of the direction of the question or even the purpose of it—it must always be defined in terms of the search for origins, but they can never be located, so the ground continues to shift, undermining man's position as the dominator of the question. If we are indeed thrown into the world, to conceive of ourselves as the creator of questions is regularly to assault the value of our creations, for the genetic question always comes up short, always fails to address that which it is supposed to resolve.

It is possible to see questions coming from man, then, but the value of looking at them that way increasingly seems suspect. More pragmatically, if we ask ourselves how we actually formulate questions, we should also begin to wonder where the idea that man had control over his queries came from. Linguistically, it is possible to say something like "I have a question I should like to raise," and such a locution suggests ownership and control, the role we like to think we have. But such remarks always occur in response to something—we have just listened to a lecture, say, and do not understand one of the key points, so we ask a question. Obviously, the question itself comes in response to something over which we had no control—the lecture—and it also suggests something else over which we have no control—the fact that we did not understand something. Now it could be said that we possess the lack of understanding, and our possession of it leads to our question, which in turn suggests control over the question, but then we have to ask ourselves how we can possess something we lack—understanding—and how the possession of that lack leads us to possess the question that arises from it. It might be preferable to see the question as presenting itself to us because of something enigmatic that we have confronted about which we should like to know more. To do so is to concede one's lack of power over the question.

There are certainly other locutions that uncover the power of the question—we say at times that the question "came" to us or "just came" to us. We say a question just occurred to us, suggesting that we do not know quite where it came from. These forms of expression concede our lack of power and reinforce Heidegger's sense of thrownness in another sense: questions seem to be thrown up at us, and even the unpalatable regurgitative assumptions in that phrase reinforce the intrusion of the question into a system that did not generate it itself. We can thus ask the question "Where do questions come from?" and seek to trace their origins within our minds, but we have seen that genetic inquiries are finally futile. If we were to ask ourselves in any particular case "Where did that question come from?" we might theoretically be able to trace an origin for it that would satisfy us. We could think about it for a while and decide that, "Oh, yes, yesterday I was doing this, and that led me today to ask about this." But while such answers may satisfy us temporarily, we need always to ask whether that one incident alone was a sufficient cause for the question, and knowing the complexity of human behavior as we do, we can never finally be satisfied with such simplistic responses. Sooner or later we must confess that we do not know quite where any particular question came from, nor where questions in general come from. Because they come to us, we always arrive too late to discover their origins.

The only way in which we can sensibly ask the question "Where do questions come from?" is to begin by conceding the impossibility of a genetic answer. It is true that Heidegger himself conceives of an origin for man's questions—Being— but even that origin is questionable, and it does not satisfy our genetic impulses in any case. To say that Being throws up questions to man through language and thus allows what is to emerge is to provide a genetic response of sorts, but what does it answer inasmuch as the concept of Being itself is such a complete mystery? It answers, on the face of it, little more than would the response that God puts these questions into our minds. We desire a more specific origin than that, and so it will not satisfy us. But it is the case that recursive and discursive questions present themselves to man, and if Being does not generate them, it remains true that questions present themselves because man is a particular location within the world who is aware of the fact that he is a location. The world in which we live presents questions to us on the basis of that which we fail to understand within our habitations within it, and our context within the world—and its relation to the rest of the world—is what is responsible for the questions that are presented to us.

But whereas it is the case that the question has control over us, it is equally true that we do not merely wait passively for it to arrive. Questions may "come" to us, but they do not come "out of the blue," unbidden on our part. They appear because we are willing to question, and in the willing to question we do not simply prepare ourselves for questions to arise—we seek them out, we will them, and we also provide the context for the particular formulation of them. In willing the question, we are also bringing to it the understanding that our context in the world essentially is, and so we are always participatory locations within the event of the question even if we are not the origin of it. The value of our participation in turn resides in the fact that we are particular locations, for the question that is framed in terms of our context always brings something to light that would not be available from another site. True to the sense of *aletheia,* that which is brought to light so particularly also conceals something that might emerge in another place, but then that is why we bring questions to others, and it is also why we continue to question as our location in the world changes: the change of locale frames our earlier query by bringing to the fore something that was hidden in the previous inquiry and sets it in a new light.

While I have been speaking about our locations in terms of the world in which we find them, it is also true that they are locations on the earth, in Heidegger's sense of the term. If the world is the human construct we allow to emerge out of the questions we ask of the earth, there is still a definable sense in which the earth exists within the world that has emerged from it. We always test our questions by placing them back in the world, and if there were only world and no earth, there would be no way adequately to discern the value of the questions we were asking. We can test the value of our world only because there is an earth. We do, for example, have bodies that are not purely worldly constructs, and we know this because we regularly test the limits, capabilities, and tolerances of the body. On the basis of our questions, we learn about some of the physical strengths and weaknesses of our bodies; we learn what forms of sustenance are and are not capable of maintaining our bodies in a fitting form, and while these kinds of questions clearly have worldly components to them—our world in part determines what kinds of food are available and what physical tests our bodies will be presented with—still the major factor in such tests is the earthly element and what it allows us to do. Regardless of the fact that we are thoroughly incapable ever of understanding the earth as earth, regardless of the fact that our world is essentially a world of language, there remains a testable com-

ponent of the earth in all our queries, and it is the testing of
it that ultimately confirms or denies the value of the world
we have allowed to emerge.

Even such seemingly worldly conceptions as fashion—how
to clothe the body—have earthly components in them, not
only because the materials, both organic and synthetic, have
emerged from the earth, but also because of what they clothe,
how well they clothe it, what kinds of social interaction are
possible within a particular set of clothes, and what the consequences are of the social interaction, from the results of particular sexual attractions to the business deals that are made
within them. The world cannot escape the earth no matter
how hard man tries to make it so; the earth refuses to disappear despite our magic, and it always returns most forcefully
when our magic fails to respond to the queries the earth
presents it with. Nor should we want it any other way inasmuch as it is the cross-fertilization between world and earth
that allows the new of the earth to emerge just as it allows
the new of the world to come forward. The world by itself is
that single-cell animal intent on forever genetically replicating
itself; the world and the earth in conjunction lead to a mixing
of genes and allow the new to present itself to us again and
again.

As one who is thrown into the world, man always finds his
questions preceding him and must place himself under them,
and if this were not obvious when we confront the origin of
questions, it should at least be clear once we have investigated
the pathway of the question itself, for questions always lead
us where they want to go—we may stop questioning if we do
not like the line of inquiry, or we may even forcibly try to alter
the direction, but we cannot finally change the path a question
chooses to take. We are led by it, we follow it to see where it
will take us, and we all know this: the scientist sees it as he
frames his questions about the world; we are aware of it when
we see where questions lead us in conversation or even when
we are thinking alone. If the question did not lead us, we
would always already know where we were going, and if we
knew where we were headed, there would be no point to the
query. We follow the question because it takes us where we

cannot go without it, and if it is a good question, it always brings to the fore something that was unexpected. That is indeed why we question: to uncover the unexpected, to bring to light that which was unknown.

Questions have their power over us because they do take us where we cannot go without them, and it is for this reason that the question always also questions man. It does so most obviously in that any query of value allows what is to emerge in a new light, and every new unconcealing also sheds light on the man who questioned in the first place. Just as we can speak of the values that emerge from the kinds of questions Heidegger asks, so too we can say that man's values emerge from the kinds of questions he asks. The question questions man by asking him what kinds of inquiries he is capable of undertaking, and it tests him by the strength of his responses to the queries he finds himself confronted with. The question takes the measure of man while man measures through the question, and it is the test of the question that is at issue when we confront the different modes of inquiry that are found in a Nietzsche or a Heidegger. For there can be no doubt that the recursive queries of Nietzsche and Heidegger seriously call into question the value of the discursive mode of inquiry; there can be no doubt that the recursive question finds the discursive one to be an inadequate measure of man and his position in the world; and in Nietzsche's case there can be no doubt that the discursive question is seen as a weakness in man, a failure to measure up to the test that the question confronts man with. It is equally true on the other side that many see Nietzsche's and Heidegger's questions as signs of weakness, as marks of the madman or of one who failed to be hardheaded enough to ask the truly serious questions. On both sides of the issue, the world and the strength of humans to ask the right questions are at stake, so it is no minor issue we are dealing with here. And for this reason if no other we must probe a bit further into the recursive question to discern the openness and the limit that it presents man with and to learn what values of man are embodied in it.

3 The Openness of Limit and the Limit of Openness

To speak of the openness of the question is to suggest a crucial difference between discursive and recursive inquiries. A discursive question is inherently self-limiting, and hence closed, both because it has a specific end in view and because the answer is usually embodied in the question itself. The specificity of the query limits the terrain it encompasses from the beginning, and while it is possible to string together long series of these questions, the basic purpose of each one is to resolve the specific issue embodied in it. The apparatus of science is developed at one level through an extensive series of discrete, linear questions, yet at another level the crucial advancements that occur within science are the result of the larger, recursive questions that generate the discursive series.

For the recursive question, on the other hand, openness is what gives it its force, the agreement to follow it where it will go without the expectation of a specific answer at the end of the inquiry. This openness, however, is based on establishing other limits. Most generally, the recursive assumes the limit of human finitude—questions do not lead man outside of himself, nor is their goal the transcendence of the human. They seek rather to inform the human by limiting queries to what man is actually capable of doing. The finitude of man is the limit not only of each man's ultimate death, but more specifically the limit of the context within which one always finds oneself. Rather than seeking to escape context, the recursive is based on the proposition that understanding can only be arrived at *through* the local situation. Hans-Georg Gadamer put the matter most succinctly when he argued that understanding, interpretation, and application should not be seen as different, sequential acts, but rather as simultaneous aspects of the same process. The discursive seeks to keep the three separate, for that allows one to argue for the purity of the moment of understanding: one first comes to understand something; having done that, one seeks an appropriate language of interpretation for that which one has understood; having arrived at a particular interpretation of one's understanding, one can then proceed to apply that which one has already understood and interpreted. This mode of reasoning is clearly based on the kinds of self-limiting questions extending in a discursive series to which I have already referred. The virtue of the model is that it does suggest that one's understanding transcends context—the moment is not corrupted by the contextualizing of a particular language or by a particular application. The linear nature of the sequences also guarantees the kind of repeatability that discursive thought requires and is sustained by the belief in definitive truths that can be arrived at through this process.

The difficulty with this formulation is that it seems that understanding is a part of, rather than anterior to, language. And if this is the case—if there is no understanding that takes place outside of language—then understanding is of necessity also interpretation, for one can only understand that for which one has words, and the words themselves are a contextual interpretation of that which is understood. Equally, while we like to think that we apply our interpretations after they have been formulated, in fact the process of formulation itself is the most crucial form of application, for to interpret something is to have applied it to one's own context in order to arrive at the formulation of that which is interpreted. The acceptance of finitude that goes along with the openness of the question, then, is based on our boundness to context and our inability ever to escape thoroughly that location out of which our questions arise to begin with.

Another way of phrasing the basis of this finitude is to say that one must accept the circularity of the questioning process from the beginning. The goal of the circles of recursivity is not to escape them but rather to make use of them, and they can best be made use of if one agrees to question within the limit of the circle. This means that the purpose of the questioning is not to bring it to a conclusion but to continue it—the end of questioning is the questioning itself, and the openness toward the world upon which an inquiring attitude is based. The end of the questioning is also to learn better how to ask questions, to discover which questions most need to be asked, and to discern how to follow the rhythms of the queries that present themselves.

Pragmatically, the openness of questioning is based on finitude because one's questions can only be open if one accepts rather than fights against one's finitude. The value of discursivity in this sense is that it appears to provide a bulwark against finitude, a protective barrier that guards against both the prejudgments of particular contexts and also, at least hypothetically, posits the possible transcendence of mortality as well. Such questions are closed precisely because they are designed to protect one from the incursions of a corrupt and corrupting world, and thus they are always inherently directed toward the ego and reinforced by the repetition compulsion that is part of the ego's defense against its limitations. In accepting the inevitable aspects of one's position in the world, one can open oneself outward to the world without feeling the need to protect oneself. One accepts the possibility of risk in doing so, but in taking account of one's limits one is better able to avoid the risks as well.

The openness of questioning is also based on the limit of understanding itself. Because a question always conceals at the same time that it unconceals, there is no way ever to arrive at the end of understanding, for each question leads into another. Because that which is brought to light always obscures something else through its brilliance, the question must always turn back on itself. Because a question always emerges through the prejudgments of a context, the prejudgments themselves always need to be questioned anew, as they are in their application through the query.

Within and through these basic limits, the question provides an openness for inquiry that is simply not possible with self-limiting, discursive inquiries. Indeed, the chief difficulty of this openness seems to be that it is *too* open, for that is one of the things against which man has been fighting for millennia. In putting an end to the final, definitive truth, the recursive seems to make anything possible, certainly a view that connects at times to the work of Nietzsche. Even if the proclamation that "God is dead" was not a boast of the conqueror but an assertion of the end of definitive truth, Nietzsche regularly is construed as an advocate of nihilism and the total relativity of truth. This leads some to revile him and others to celebrate him, but in both cases the reactions are misplaced, for the openness of the recursive question does not lead to the relativity of everything. As is the case with the thought of the eternal return and the deliverance from revenge, "God is dead" is meant to mark a limit of human understanding that is designed to prevent the intrusion of relativism through the use of God. The limit of "God is dead" is thus a call to responsibility rather than a proclamation of freedom from truth. In liberating us from our illusions of static and eternal verities, Nietzsche has not made everything possible; he has prevented us from making anything possible through the proclamation of eternal truth.

If Nietzsche were indeed devoted to a world of relativity, why would he try to bear the thought of the eternal return? As a mere test of the human will to will? Or was it rather to delineate the conditions under which the relativity of truth can be avoided? Why would Nietzsche be concerned that man should be delivered from his desire for revenge and his revulsion against time if he were devoted to nihilism? Surely to a nihilist it makes little difference whether the truth and values of the world continue to be determined by the spirit of revenge or not. Nietzsche seeks to overcome the relativity of truth by establishing the limits through which it can be arrived at, and as such, "God is dead" is as essential as being delivered from revenge or accepting the eternal return. Each of these conceptual formulations is designed to make man turn away from his revulsion against time as it seeks to invert the Kantian Ideas of limit. Each of them is designed to show how man generates nihilism through his revulsion against time. They are the conditions of our humanity rather than the negation of it, as any careful reading of Nietzsche would show.

Heidegger's work is complementary to Nietzsche's in this regard because he more unmistakably shows how the openness of limit also has the limit of openness. One cannot freely hurl oneself toward the future without regard for the consequences, as the nihilists would have it. Nor is one free to invent the world as one chooses, as many existentialists at one time argued. The view of the former is simply a helpless expression of the aesthetic devoid of truth while the latter is an even more hopeless fabrication of the real in the belief that anything is real if one says it is. The limit of openness forces one to submit oneself to the openness of the question, and far from giving one any ultimate kind of freedom, this submission forces one to go where one is led. No question is free of direction, and to respond to it is to agree to follow it in accordance with the context in which it arises. On the pathway of the question the possibilities are limited from the outset by the implications inherent in the inquiry. This does not mean that the answer is inherent in the question, for there are any number of possibilities suggested by it, and no one questioner could ever hope to cover them all. But a query is open only because it sets a limit—thought is possible only because one always begins someplace—and that limit is what sets one on the path away from relativism and toward provisional truth. In this way, a good question is much like individual life itself. One is born with certain limits, but they provide the basis for innumerable possibilities. The possibilities the world presents us with lead to choices that in one sense limit one further, but in another sense make openness all the more possible.

It may be the case, for example, that maturity in our culture is often greeted with a sense of despair whenever it comes— it seems to have been moved forward and is now marked by what has come to be called the "midlife crisis"—largely because it denotes an individual's awareness that his basic pathways in life are already established and that the only thing left to do seems to be to fill in the blanks to the end of the already established line. This can be all the more disappointing when it is contrasted with the heady days of youth when everything seemed possible because one had not yet come to understand the pathways one was on. The limits of the possible seem to have become so constricted that life no longer bears any excitement. But this is true only to the extent that one takes ignorance for possibility and understanding for limitation. There is indeed a limit in maturity, and it is understanding, but rather than foreclosing the possibilities of the future, it opens them up, for one comes to know what one can do, what one is most capable of exploring, and what is most likely to be worth exploring. The limit of understanding narrows the range of possibilities in one sense, but it really expands them because the solidity of orientation that maturity offers allows one a more secure footing in the world, which in turn allows one to pursue those things that are most worth going after.

The same is true for the question. Like a human birth, no query begins innocently—it comes dripping with the odor of the context from which it arose, and that situation provides the opening and the limit to the direction of the inquiry. But the more we pursue the question, the more we find ourselves submitting to the direction it chooses to take. This is perhaps most obvious in the kinds of conversation in which one wonders how one ended up arguing what one is arguing. One begins on the path of the question with a certain idea of where one is going to go with it, yet one is often surprised to find where one has been led. And when one finds oneself moving in a direction quite different from the one one thought one was going in, the sense of being manacled to the question, the sense of being caught in the grip of that for which one was unprepared, is not simply an illusion based on the drama of discussion. The question has overtaken one's idea of where it should go and directed one there in spite of oneself.

Socrates called the dialectic of questioning "divine wandering" in the *Cratylus*, and that is a formulation of the path of the question that needs attending to because it seems so thoroughly to articulate the matter. The openness of the question does indeed lead to a kind of wandering, first because one is never sure where the question is going to lead, second because the lack of a specific answer to the query makes the path wider than it is with self-limiting questions. One then does wander, but not aimlessly—the wandering is divine, both because it divines the truth and because it is directed from outside oneself. We may no longer think that the gods oversee the pathways of our questions, but the divination comes from without and is outside of our control. Far from being aimless or relative, the question is directed from without and goes where it will, taking us with it unless we resist its sway.

The question does lead us, but this does not mean that we cannot stop along the way to see where we have come and how we got there. The recursive query has built into it these loops of return that question the pathway one is on, and they are an essential aspect of reinforcing and expanding the value of the question's path. Divine wandering does not mean mindless wandering any more than it means that one is incapable of questioning the nature of the path. One must instead regularly ask how one got where one did and attempt to discern the implications of one's being there. In one sense these questionings are wanderings off of the path, or digressions from its main line, but more importantly they flesh out the consequences of the path and thus further confirm or deny the value of being on it. When one speaks of the power of ideas or the intoxication of thought, one is conceding their force to lead us, but at the same time one does not grant them the rights of totalitarian regimes. One always bring one's own context to the question and thus helps to provide a shape to it, and the context is always based on that which one has understood prior to the question. It is, then, not only the question which puts one's understanding at issue; it is also one's understanding that places the value of the question on the line. The dialectical relationship between the two maintains the pathway and limits the power of the question over us.

The discipline of the question, however, does not assure us of the truth any more than it necessarily leads us away from relativism, for we have our own stake in its pathway and our own interest in its direction—if we did not there would be no point in placing ourselves under its sway to begin with. But the question does have a methodology of its own, contrary to the belief that only the laws of reason are a fitting guarantee for thought and its consequences, and the methodology has the further benefit that it is not value-free but rather value-full. One does not first determine the value of the logic of the question and then attend to the specifics of the issue, for from the recursive view there would never be an adequate way to separate the logic of the question and its specific formulation. The values and the logic are inseparable aspects of one another, the differential equation that marks the context of the question and determines its validity. Traditionally the value of logic is seen as a means of testing the coherence of a line of inquiry and is thus in part designed to separate rhetoric from logic in the hope of using logic to distinguish the "merely" rhetorical aspects of the argument. Logic was the weapon to be employed against the rhetoricians to reveal their deceits, but the separation of logic and rhetoric only expanded the powers of the rhetoricians, for it is perfectly possible to construct a logical series of questions that is also diabolical in intent, and logic is powerless to deal with such cases. Only by arguing for the inseparability of logic and rhetoric can one hope to address this problem, as should be more than obvious when we see how traditional philosophy in this century has moved from the hope of finally underpinning the base of logic in mathematics to doing things with words, a radically diminished view of the value of logic itself.

If logic is inseparable from rhetoric, we need to ask what kind of logic this is, for its binding to context suggests a clear difference from the more traditional forms. It is first of all based on the principle of exclusion. Inasmuch as each question does arise out of a particular context, both the context and the question establish from the outset the range of possible responses. If, for example, one is asking about the nature of a poem, the possibilities of response are limited by the opening question one asks. One may ask what the poem is about and proceed to evaluate its language in terms of what it says, bringing to bear on the question the specific thematic material of the poem, the use of sound and meter within it, the form and the structure of it, and the historical context out of which it came. In so doing, one might provide a wholly satisfactory answer to the question at the same time that one reveals through exemplification what one sees embodied in the nature of poetry. In formulating the issue this way, the logic of the question would be based on the idea that a poem is indeed about something, and thus the explanation proffered would be a test of this logic as well, for to the extent that one was satisfied with the description of the poem, to the extent that one felt the data of the poem were fully dealt with through the question, one would find the logic valid.

To ask this question of a poem, though, is to exclude several other possibilities. If one proceeded according to the question of what the poem is about, one would exclude the possibility that poetry is not about anything, that its function is not to have a theme or a definable purpose but merely to be what it is. That which is concealed in the question of what poetry is about is the possibility that it is about nothing per se—that it is part of the world rather than about it. Thus, one might just as easily ask how the poem works and end up with a different series of responses to what it does that are wholly consistent with the context of the question, yet which at the same time exclude the possibility that the poem is about anything at all. One could also, of course, ask either question and end up encompassing the other, but the other would still be encompassed according to the logic of the opening query. One might begin with the question of what the poem is about and conclude finally that it is about the way it is a part of the world rather than a commentary on it just as one might ask how the poem works and ultimately show that everything within it develops the theme of mutability or whatever.

Nevertheless, the question of what the poem is about has built into it a series of assumptions about aboutness of the kind that we would not find present in the questioning of something else. We would not be likely to ask what a rock is about, for we assume that it is about nothing, though we may be inclined to ask what its functions are. Likewise, to ask how a poem works is to adopt the technician's attitude, is to assume that the poem has more in common with a machine than it does with a treatise on the nature of truth or a manual on how to construct a bomb shelter. It is seen not as a program for action but rather as a mode of action itself. The questions themselves have a logic built into their orientation and attitude, and while one of the goals of questioning is to test the value of that logic, the logic itself is irrefragable once one picks it up. If one decides that the technician's attitude toward poetry fundamentally mistakes the nature of a poem, one must change the logic by changing the question, for the consistency of the logic of the technician cannot be changed in any material way without interfering with the basic logic itself.

It should also be evident that the logic embodied in the question is affected by the historical context as well. It would not have occurred to a critic one hundred years ago to ask a technician's question about the nature of poetry, though the question of what the poem is about would doubtless arise. In thus asking about the logic that is inherent in any particular rhetorical context, we come to see that it is not merely being tested with respect to its value for a particular poem—it is also being tested as a fitting response to the historical context that generated it. If one follows the logic of the question to its end, one sees in this particular instance that it is the logic of the technician, and that in turn makes us consider whether the logic of the technician is appropriate to a consideration of the nature of poetry. It makes us ask whether the logic that treats a poem like a machine and a critic like a man in a white lab coat really addresses the nature of the poem itself. As a result, one tests the logic of the question both through its application—how well it works on the job at hand—and through the recursivity inherent in it, the returns within the question that lead one to ask why it was framed the way it was, what one expects to learn from putting the matter that way, and how adequate a logic we find in the premises underlying the question. The rhetoric of the question is quite logical in its own way, and its logic is also testable at any number of levels from the question of the value of the orientation to its applicability in particular contexts to the fruits of the labor involved to the perspective it suggests of the questioner himself. One could thus deny the force of the logic by concluding that a poem is not like a machine, by deciding that not very much is gained by seeing it that way, by concluding that the critic's role is not that of a technician, or by seeing that in a particular investigation of a poem something important is left out when one has exhaustively explored the possibilities inherent in the question.

The function of a question is not simply to provide an orientation toward something through the logic it brings to bear on it. It is also designed to question the logic of the orientation itself—the testing of the logic as applied to a particular situation also calls into question the orientation, for if the responses that the logic generates are seen to be less than adequate, the orientation is as susceptible to questioning as is the particular thing being questioned. In this way, the boundaries of the logic of the query establish the line of thought one must take if one is to follow it, but they are also being probed for their value. We are able to arrive at some kind of understanding to begin with because the logic excludes an entire range of possible responses, but the understanding we arrive at will lead us to question whether or not that which was excluded should have been. All questions limit our freedom by telling us where to go, and that is why they have value to begin with, but they should also prompt us to ask whether we agree with the imposed limits.

Far from leading to relativism, then, the openness of the recursive question prevents it from entering into our speculation. Far from leaving us with a series of indiscriminate orientations to adopt, it forces us to question the value of orientations and to learn how to choose among them. And far from leaving us no valid way of choosing among the orientations, the open question allows us to consider seriously for the first time the question of the value of orientation. Without the recursive view, the perspective is always constructed in terms of an escape from orientation, a flight from involvement in the values of the questions we pose, for that is indeed the goal behind a value-free conception of questions. And as long as we consider a value-free orientation to be our goal, we shall never be able adequately to address the question of value or the question of the values inherent in the notion of value-free inquiry that we so desperately seek to hold onto.

The problem of the value-free question is made more difficult by the rhetoric that surrounds the debate, for the goal of a value-free mode of inquiry is the cornerstone of what we call humanism, and those humanists who uphold the virtues of value-freeness not only argue that it is the foundation of all values; they also have the club of humanism to wield against those who do not share their view—to say that one is not a humanist within this circle is to suggest that one is *anti*human, against humanity, as though the only way one could have a concern for man would be through the ideology of humanism. But if we see humanism for what it is, a man-centered orientation to the world that is based on the notion of a value-free mode of questioning, it should be clear that it by no means follows that one is against humanity if one calls into question the goal of a value-free orientation. I have already argued that the grail of a value-free system is a reflection of man's revulsion against time, and that it is connected to the repetition compulsion of the death instinct rather than the life instinct. Equally, I have argued that there is an irremediable gap between value-freeness and values, that one cannot begin from a value-free perspective and move into a value-full perspective, that there is not a logical bridge between the two positions. Likewise, I have argued that the result of this gap between value-freeness and value-fullness leads one to defer infinitely the question of value. If the value-free perspective excludes from the very beginning the question of man's revulsion against time, how could it ever hope to lead to a consideration of the revulsion that led to the ideal of the value-free goal to begin with? It could only consider it by accepting the fact that it itself is based on that revulsion and is thus not value-free at all, that, on the contrary, its values are the negation of value through the denial of the revulsion upon which value-free inquiry is based. Likewise, the law of non-contradiction upon which value-free inquiry is built establishes from the outset the impossibility of arriving at values because it denies that they can emerge from the contradictions inherent in man. It assumes that the good does not emerge against, yet in consort with, the evil that is inherent in man; it assumes that one can separate the categories of good and evil and deal with them independently of each other without ever considering the possibility that the good only emerges through a questioning of the evil that we seek to distinguish from it. In excluding the possibility of the inseparability of the two, value-freeness is forced always to assume that the logic of good is different from the logic of evil and that the logic of evil is indeed amenable to a value-free exposition.

From this perspective, value-freeness may be the affirmation of humanism, but it is also the denial of the human, or at least a good part of it. The project of a value-free system of analysis is simply another way of avoiding the problems of the human, another attempt to escape the consequences of our own nature. In Sophocles' time, the human might have been avoided through a conception of fate that left the eruptions of evil in the world in the hands of the gods, and value-free goals seem totally unrelated to such evasions of the human. But while the explanations of reason might seem more sophisticated than a theory of fate, the consequences are the same: an avoidance of the human. Humanism is devoted to the powerful truth that one of the strongest desires of humanity is to avoid confronting its own nature. Humanism seeks to tame the "undesirable" aspects of human nature by developing a platform above the contingencies of life that would allow man to investigate the contingencies without being susceptible to them. This is why those who say that science is our grail and our religion say more than they know, for it is not merely that we have devoted ourselves to its descriptions of the world in which we live; more importantly, through its descriptions we can avoid the issue of our humanity by saying that we are working toward a rational explanation of it. Science is that articulation of reality that allows us infinitely to defer the question of man's place and value in the world, and if humanists think they are working against the grain of science in seeking to restore a human face to the world, they ought to ask themselves whether their own goals are not based on the role of the technician that scientists adopt.

We see the results of the attitude of the value-free most obviously in the realm of science, but they are present throughout human endeavors in the West, as one would expect inasmuch as science is a product of humanism rather than separate from it. And scientific endeavors are most applicable because they demonstrate that the problem is not that man does not care about value but that his mode of questioning has prevented him from addressing the question. Within the scientific, the question arises in the context of the scientist's responsibility. Is Einstein responsible for the consequences of the atom bomb because his theories made it possible for one to be developed? Is one who investigates the nature of genes through recombinant DNA experiments responsible for the possible misuse of his findings or technique? These are the questions of value we ask, and they quickly become palpably absurd, or at least they lead to absurd consequences. If we are to say that Einstein is responsible for the atom bomb—even though he was unaware of it as a possibility—then we have effectively argued that human inquiry must come to an end, for one can never be certain about its consequences. This is absurd because it makes no sense to hold someone responsible for unforeseen consequences, but it is equally absurd to assume that we could declare an end to human inquiry if we wanted to. Man will continue to ask questions regardless of the prohibitions against the activity, so any such prohibition would be pointless. A government could deny one access to the means of inquiry, but this would simply prompt the inquirer to find a way to work around the prohibition.

If it is absurd to make an Einstein responsible for consequences he never foresaw or did not intend, then the logic of the value-free system tells us that inasmuch as his inquiry is scientific to begin with, these questions of value should never come up in the first place. The scientist's considerations do not fall within the range of values, so if we are to look for responsibility in these matters, we must turn in another direction. Of course the matter becomes somewhat murkier when the scientist no longer simply develops theories but also specifically seeks to employ them in something like the construction of an atom bomb, but then the scientist is not the one who will make the bomb itself, nor will he make the decision actually to employ it, so his activity once again must be construed as value-free. This in turn defers the issue of value to the technocrats who are responsible for the specific construction of the bomb and the development of the contexts that will make its implementation possible, but the same arguments of value-freeness apply to their work—they are not making choices of value; they are merely making use of their expertise. We could follow the chain of logic all the way to its end, which would presumably be somewhere like the White House or the Kremlin, though the president, while he would doubtless concede that his use of the bomb was not a value-free choice, would doubtless also maintain that his choice of value was dictated to him by events in another sphere over which he had no control, and the regress would continue.

Regardless of the end of the chain, we would all probably concede that somewhere along the way from Einstein to the president, the question of value intruded itself and had to be dealt with. The difficulty is that in considering each link of the chain, we could always show reasons why value did not enter in and thus should not be considered. We could not really locate the moment when values intruded in any but an arbitrary way because each step, considered in itself, could be seen to be based on value-free decisions and thus devoid of responsibility. So we would face a dilemma: we could conclude that no one was responsible for the chain of events— we could certainly not ever locate the origin of the chain, for in this case it was clearly not Einstein who began it—or that everyone had to assume a share of the responsibility. If we were to conclude that no one was responsible, then we would have to infer that values come in from the outside, that they intruded on the situation through some extrahuman means— perhaps the gods, or fate—which would clearly be absurd. But if we were to conclude that everyone was responsible, we would be contradicting ourselves, for we had decided at the outset that Einstein could not be held responsible for that about which he did not know. Even if we concluded we were wrong in absolving Einstein of complicity, universal responsibility would in effect absolve everyone and simply put the question out of play altogether. If everyone is responsible, then no one has to take his responsibility very seriously, for the only way he could do so would be to take on others' responsibility as well, and one cannot really do that. By beginning from a perspective that assumes one can make value-

free choices, one eliminates the possibility of specifically dealing with the intrusion of values into the context at any level.

The next seemingly logical step on this road would be to
conclude that the question of value is there from the beginning, that scientific inquiry is never value-free, and that therefore we ought to question the values of science itself. The
problem with the assumption that science is not a value-free
enterprise is that it is a position usually adopted by those who
are totally against science, who see it as inimical to every
human and natural activity. The shrill cries from this camp
equally fail to address the issue of science and its values;
instead, the antiscientific community isolates the negative
consequences of some scientific pursuit—nuclear power,
chemical pollution, and the like—and argues that science
always leads to the inimical, that nothing good results from
inquiries of a scientific nature. This is readily enough visible
as a variation on the theme that science is responsible for
everything that emerges from it, and inasmuch as nothing
good comes from it, we ought to have done with it altogether.
No illumination of the values of science is possible from such
a view, for it fails to address the question and simply argues
that science is pure evil.

If we are seriously to consider the values of science, we
must begin with the assumption that it has them, but not that
they are necessarily either good or bad. This means that we
cannot assume that only what man does with science has to
do with values, and it also means that we must see the values
of science as an expression of man. While science is applied
to the natural world, its values are involved in its manner of
application and need to be considered in that light. From this
vantage point, it must be assumed that science, like other
human enterprises, is faced with the limiting nature of its
questions. All scientific queries bring things to light but also
conceal other things in the process: it is impossible to maintain
the big-bang theory of the origin of the universe while also
believing that the universe is in a steady state. The illumination of the one view precludes the possibilities of the other.
This is precisely why science is not value-free in any sense:
its questions are as double-edged as any other kind, and

they are always framed in the context of some extrascientific metaphor that is also an embodiment of values. These values are there at the beginning as much as they are there at the end. Science may, for example, construct a cosmological theory that all life eventually dies and characterize it in terms of entropy, but the values in the theory are not simply derived from an older human conception of existence—they also affect the attitude toward present existence, as the plethora of uses of "entropy" that crop up in the most unusual of social contexts suggests. Any cosmological theory embodies a conception of life, and the values of that theory are found not only in the questions science asks but are also disseminated to the larger social apparatuses as well.

The traditional commentaries on science manage to express some of the central values in the way man has come to practice it, though it is questionable whether they are intrinsic to it or not. Our visions of mad scientists and the like do nevertheless reveal that we conceive of science as the one business where it is still possible to imagine ourselves in a godlike role. Events on the sociocultural level over the past hundred years have put an end to any illusions on our part that human nature is of itself moving toward any inevitable, perfectible whole, regardless of the presence of debased models of Marxian thought that still exist. But through science—again, because it is conceived of as value-free and neutral—we can still hold out the hope that we might yet reach the land of perfectibility. The will to become god that is at the heart of the death instinct still reigns strongly here. Science, in this sense, is the dominant form of expression in our time not only because it has transformed the earth so radically but also because these radical transformations allow us to imagine that our vision of ourselves may yet come to pass. The view of a perfect world with a perfected, immortal man seems essential to our way of viewing the value and the values of science. We will forgive any number of atrocities in its name so long as we can hold that vision a bit longer. This we might construe as the traditional view of the values of science.

Increasingly, though, science has turned against that grand vision. We were enamored of its power, yet that power began to take on a frightening hue when it no longer seemed under our control. The great, rational machine of science seemed to turn into a behemoth that stalked the corners of the globe looking for fresh things to devour. Not that most of us are inclined to speak of science in that way, but underneath our speculations about it resides the fear of human destructiveness that we seem all too willing to transpose onto science precisely because of its seeming power over us—this is the modern vision of the fates that the gods bring to us. And when science the deliverer becomes science the devourer, we must again reevaluate the image of man that goes along with our view of it. If science has come increasingly to harbor the vision of evil that some people always found in it, though, it is not that science is really evil, but rather that we have seriously misjudged just what it is, and sensing that misjudgment, we are now more inclined to turn on the former savior of ourselves. In failing to see that we invested science with the value of deliverer, we now fail to see that once it cannot deliver, like any good king, it is also the most likely place to turn for a scapegoat, so it becomes the devourer. But we have learned nothing if we simply invert the values we have invested in science.

This series of events is also ironic in that it was often those who were most vocally against the invasion of science and most willing to see it as devourer who were also responsible for spreading its values to other domains. Certainly, for example, the New Criticism in America was based on strongly antiscientific rhetoric, yet at the same time the New Critic's greatest success was to turn our attitude toward poetry in the direction of the technician's view. Resisting the technicians of science—precisely at a time when scientists began to see that they were not the technicians they thought they were—the New Critics became the technicians of poetry. They were artful technicians, to be sure, and much was gained from their technical insights, but their views were dominated by the science they so despised, and by a science that had already begun to move away from the values that seemed so despicable.

What the changes in attitude toward science ought to suggest to us is neither a view of it as deliverer or devourer, neither of the scientist as godlike technician nor as evil magician; rather, they ought to show how we have projected our own values onto science without directly considering what values it does have and what values we ought to bring to it. At base, the values of science are embodied as much in the questions it asks as in the methodology through which it pursues the answers, and they are both modest and open. They are designed to open up our understanding of the world and our positions within it and are based on the premise that all questions return, but that every time they return there is more understanding in them. Science did, after all, emerge from philosophy and its own recursive questions, and it did not leave its philosophical component behind when it came to occupy its own special terrain. At the basic level of the question, of the hypothesis and the theory, science has always been recursive, even if it was not always aware of its recursivity, and it has always been open, even if it did at times see its goal as the closing-up of the world in the perfection of death. Science as the inquiry into the nature of what is has always held at its center the values inherent in the growth and production of life rather than its elimination or its preservation in death through the infinite repetitions of regression. We are the ones who, when our own idea of our powers and values changed, began to transpose them onto science; we are the ones who have taken scientific inquiry and tried to turn it against its own openness.

Of course, we did not begin to realize this until the metaphor of the world-as-machine began to break down and along with it our ideas of ourselves as master craftsmen. The openness of scientific inquiry was made evident when this shift began to take place, for when it confirmed our inability ever to escape our rootedness to the earth, and when it denied the simplicity and the power of the machine metaphor, there was no guarantee that science would be able to maintain its own status when the seeming principles upon which it was founded were undermined. No one knew that the world of relativity physics would generate still more powerful forces; it might instead have turned science as a discipline and mode of inquiry into one having no more importance than philosophy has today. It was in the interests of science and of the scientist in one sense to preserve the stability of the world that was called into question by its own inquiries, yet its openness prevailed over the changes that it inaugurated despite the possible consequences for itself. There is, of course, no doubt that science has as a result more dominance than ever before, both because its new descriptions of the world were more powerful and because they led science into ever more obscure corners that have made it into a religion that only those who are willing to give their lives to its service could hope to master. That, however, was not evident a hundred years ago, and the reverse possibility could also theoretically have happened.

The questions of science are clearly not inimical to life, then, but there is also the issue of scientific methodology and its values. Is the experimental method itself problematic in terms of the values it reveals, if we assume that it is a method of establishing conditions of reproducibility in order to introduce variables into those conditions to determine the effect of the variables on the situation? Is the reproducibility of scientific method the reproducibility of the repetition-compulsion and the death instinct? One would have to say that it is not, for the goal of scientific reproducibility is not to retain the repetition of the same. On the contrary, the reproducibility is established always in order to understand the effect of the intrusion of difference into it, what happens when the eruption of difference alters the repetition of the same. The goal of the experimental method is once again to open up and out, to take in new differences and see what emerges through the introduction of them. It is an expansive method rather than a restrictive one, and its goal is always to open out to the new on the basis of what is already known.

If the values of the scientific question and its methodology are not suspect, however, that does not mean that they cannot be put to use in bad ways. If the scientific question is designed to open up our understanding of the world, science can still be used for purely manipulative purposes with the egocentric desires of man in control. Likewise, if the purpose of scientific methodology is to open up the world, that does not mean it cannot be used for other purposes. And if those potentialities for abuse were not inherent in science, man's perpetual forgetfulness would doubtless lead to abuses of science in any case. One does not have to argue that the intent of the scientist is what is most crucially at stake here, for more often than not it is probably that which escapes the intent of the scientist that leads to the problems. If, for example, the chief virtue of the scientific method is that it allows one to study a particular variable under otherwise reproducible conditions, there is no guarantee that the site and the framework of the experiment will be remembered as a site and a framework. One might easily ignore the fact that variables occur not in reproducible circumstances as a rule or in isolable contexts. One might easily enough as a result forget to consider the possible consequences of the application of one's understanding when one places that variable back into a context in which its effects manifest their force over a much wider range of phenomena.

Similarly, it is easy enough to forget that the specific, open questions of science always feed back into a world in which the responses to those questions can have equally unforeseen consequences. Indeed, in one sense Heidegger's ceaseless questioning about the relationship between Being and beings is devoted to precisely this point. In following the pathway of science, we have forgotten along the way that beings do not live in discrete and independent contexts—the specificity of our scientific questions, combined with the metaphor of the machine, led us to think of beings solely as objects, as manipulable as interchangeable parts, with no regard for the fact that they are not discrete, isolable, independent phenomena, that they have essential, and essentially fragile, relations to other beings, and that they have the same relations to something larger than those particular beings, the earth itself. In forgetting, we have transposed the isolation of the laboratory onto the world and assumed that similar attitudes could prevail there. Here it is our forgetfulness rather than science itself or any particular scientist that has led to the kinds of unforeseen consequences that have been most deleterious to our own health and the health of the earth. And in repeatedly pointing out the fragility of these relationships—and the delicacy of our relationship to the earth—Heidegger has simply reminded us of that which we need always to remember. He has not turned against science and technology, but he has spoken out against the forgetfulness that has led us to make of science and technology what we have.

The point of this rather extensive discussion of the values of science, though, is not merely to suggest what values it has, but rather to argue that all modes of inquiry have values—are inevitably based on them—and that none of them is value-free. Only by beginning from such a standpoint can we hope to overcome the duplicities involved in the vision of value-free inquiry. For the ideal of value-freeness not only obtrudes in a negative way when we begin to consider responsibility; it is also involved in our forgetfulness of the relations of beings. Because we have assumed that what goes on in the laboratory or in scientific inquiry is value-free, we have equally assumed that the results and the application of that inquiry will be value free. Our forgetfulness of "Being," if you will, is the result of our belief that value-free inquiries do not involve questions of "Being." We have forgotten "Being" because we have chosen to, for value-free inquiry can only occur extrinsic of questions of "Being" inasmuch as these questions inevitably involve us in the passing of time through which "Being" manifests itself to us. The illusion of the value-free question is the illusion that we have the power to negate "Being," just as we are free to remove things from their context without concern for the disruption of relationships that such alterations involve; or at the very least that we have the right to eliminate such questions from our consideration. Inasmuch as the results of our inquiries have repeatedly shown us the consequences of ignoring these problems, though, we should recognize the futility of value-free inquiry and the negativity that results from the illusion of it.

We are not only speaking here of these problems in the scientific domain, for if anything the issue has been much more clearly addressed there than elsewhere. If we have yet fully to trace the consequences of our value-full scientific inquires, at least the consequences have begun to be consid-

ered. The same cannot be said for other areas of human
questioning, for there as often as not the desire for value-free
inquiry is stronger than it ever was. Carrying along with them
as they do the idea of nineteenth-century science as the proper
mode of legitimization, the "human sciences" seek all the
more strenuously to find a value-free method. Instead of
looking at the example of philosophy, which increasingly
sought to recover its lost prominence through the ever-
stronger assertion of value-free proceedings, and which, as a
result, has become increasingly insignificant as a serious
mode of inquiry, instead of looking at that more pertinent
example, the human sciences continue to try to establish
themselves on the firm ground that gave way under science
long ago. The chief danger of this is not simply that modes of
inquiry become truncated and pointless; it is rather that the
view of human nature that emerges from such questioning is
as artificial as the idea that individual electrons can be studied
thoroughly and definitively in isolation. The view of man
that is bound to emerge from these pursuits will always fail
adequately to take into account the effects of the variables it
studies on the larger human actions such accounts purport
to provide. And this is to say nothing for the basic values
embodied in the idea of value-freeness and the effect of those
values on the world. These are serious questions precisely
because no question is value-free, because all questions ultimately have effects on attitudes and orientations and the
consequences that result from them.

In this regard, it is not the sciences that are most threatening
to our world, nor their products like the atom bomb or the
profusion of noxious chemicals; the real threat is the attitude
we bring to that which we have already helped to emerge,
and that attitude cannot be dealt with by science in any of its
manifestations within the human sciences, be they the study
of the individual in isolation, of human aggregates, or of the
two together. The question of the attitude we bring to the
future we shall create is rather dependent on our inquiries
into the values we bring to our investigations, and here we
can only begin with a full examination of our commitment to
the ideal of value-free inquiry and an even fuller examination

of why we so resolutely cling to that ideal in the face of increasingly obvious evidence of its nonexistence. That examination begins with the question of what idea of man is behind such a view and with the question of what view of man is being avoided through it. Given to strategies of displacement as we are, the most pertinent inquiry would begin with that which is avoided, but inasmuch as that is intrinsically bound up with the ideal that is projected, it will inevitably be uncovered in any case once we begin to seek for the value of our procedures and techniques.

While I have suggested that we can begin to get an idea of the values we possess through a consideration of Nietzsche's, Heidegger's, and Freud's investigations, they offer us only a starting point, albeit a crucial one. We need still to consider more seriously the openings they have provided in order to see what the consequences of their thought are for us and to see if they provide us with a view of the world that can both describe for us our implication in a set of values that no longer works and present to us a pathway to a different set of values that more fully commits us to the limits that make our openness toward the world possible and to the discipline that that openness of the question provides us on the way to the values that we allow to emerge through that discipline. And in order to make use of Nietzsche, Heidegger, and Freud, we need to move backward with them as they show us how our thought arrived where it did and forward to see what the transvaluation of our values could mean in terms of the modes of inquiry that are already available to us, in the scientific world, in the world of the human sciences, and in the sociopolitical world of which we are all a part.

4 The Conflict of Questions

The inevitability of value-full questions brings to the fore-ground certain human problems that have heretofore been ignored or displaced by the concept of value-free inquiry. If we begin with questions that emerge from the difference of the context in which they are raised, we have to see our inquiries as our mode of existence rather than our way out of it, either by returning to the beginning or pushing ourselves to the end. The on-the-wayness of the question—and the values that are bound up with it—do not simply generate problems of attitude that concern our desire for the end, nor are these problems built simply on our displacement from the position of control over our questions. If these were the only difficulties, one could simply argue that we need to come to accept our position in the world rather than ceaselessly try to escape it, but while it is conceivable that we could learn to live with what we are, there is no guarantee that we could accomplish this. Too many people are committed to the belief that the greatest moments of Western civilization are the re-sults of the magnificent spirit of revenge to assure any kind of easy passageway through this difficulty. The commitment to the power of revenge—even if it is a nihilistic force—is so great that man has a hard time imagining choices that do not occur under and through its aegis. At the very outset the recursivity of difference thus needs to face the resistances of the questions of revenge, and the conflict of questions must first be determined on this ground before it is possible to confront the conflict inherent in the question of recursivity as well.

One can argue against the value-free and show how it is connected to the repetition compulsion of the death instinct and still not begin to deal with the powerful continuities that make the system run. One can equally—as writers like Foucault have done—delimit carefully the structures of power through which the force of revenge embosses itself on man, but such demonstrations do little to convince those who think they are in control. Swept up as they are in the force that comes from the denial of difference and the assertion of the same, they are hardly likely to deny the principle upon which their sense of power is seemingly founded, for in fact they are dominated by the power itself rather than having control over it. To reverse the ratio of force and location is to accept the full fearfulness of that power, and this is precisely what is being avoided through the assertion of value-freeness. In believing that one can step out of time and out of oneself, one is also committed to the notion that therefore time has no control over one and that the self is made by the will to convert it to identity by observing it from afar. Because these premises likewise generate the impression that one has the same amount of control over that which surrounds one, the world is defined in terms of the good of the self that escapes contingency. To redefine the network of relations involved here and to demonstrate the futility and destructiveness of the practice that emerges from it is a seemingly impossible task, for it could only begin with the acceptance of contingency, the acceptance of one's inescapable rootedness in time, and that is precisely what is rejected from the outset. Even more, because the reasons for the institutionalization of this practice are always displaced in order to disguise their origins in the revulsion against time and the spirit of revenge, there seems to be no mode of access into the system itself. If one confronts its stated premises, they become more tenaciously held because the terror of what lies outside them becomes more apparent. If one confronts the terror itself, it is rejected as a possibility because its displacement has already generated the blindness that prevents one from seeing it. The vicious circle of repetition and displacement only reinforces itself rather than confronts the issues at hand.

Similarly, one could seek to demonstrate the fruits of the discursive mode of inquiry, pointing to the historical, social, and physical changes that have occurred as a result of it, but any deleterious consequences are not seen as a result of discursivity but rather are construed as due to the failure of discursivity to hold full sway over everything. Because the negative is always seen as coming from without, and because discursivity is designed to eliminate it, the negativity is never understood as arising from within the discursive—it is not perceived as the failure of the discursive mode but rather as something that demonstrates the greater need for it. Again, the chain of illusion is so powerful that there seems to be no way to break outside of it, no way to crack its code in a way that would convince its practitioners that it avoids exactly what it purports to deal with. Seen from without, the reciprocity of revenge returns with ever more viciousness, reinforcing the continuities out of which man seeks to break through the discursive; seen from within, the discursive is the sole means of protection from that reciprocity that would quickly overrun the world if one did not continue to assert the validity of discursivity.

On the historical level, such breaks in reciprocity can occur, but their fruits are not necessarily guaranteed to have any longer-term effect. One could argue, for example, that the gesture of President Sadat in 1977 was such a break with the discursive, was an opening based on the denial of the spirit of revenge, but—at least as events up to the present suggest—such gestures have value in the particular context only so long as they are seen for what they are. They can equally be taken as a ruse, as an attempt to get one to put down one's guard so that the other can swiftly reinstitute the cycles of revenge. If the event is construed this way, it may still have a symbolic force, but it fails to break the grip of the circle it sought to dissolve. In international relations, there is no doubt that, as elsewhere, the recursive denial of the revulsion against time is the exception rather than the rule inasmuch as to take that step is to risk everything with the full knowledge of the power one must put off in order to step outside of the circle.

On the national level, one can see the same set of principles at work with the same kinds of justification. Once one sees that the discursive practices that delimited the zones of inclusion and exclusion within the network were established via the force of revenge and the power that derives from it, the easiest way to deal with one's own exclusion is to seize the reins of reciprocity oneself and turn them against those whose power is based on one's exclusion. Hegel's master/slave dialectic works as well today as it ever did; indeed, it works even better because more and more people have discovered its powers and have put them to use. It is not hard to see the political network of the United States as increasingly based on the dialectic of revenge, and this has occurred not simply because our media tend to present the actions within the political network in this fashion. The principle of revenge *works;* it is regularly seen to work as no other principle does; and inasmuch as it was frequently the instrument that was used upon those who were excluded, it is quite predictable that they would reciprocate in order to lift themselves out of exclusion. The problem with this cycle as it is occurring today is that there is no evidence of anyone's working against the principle, no indication of any gestures of renunciation of its power, and the effect is that the more it is instituted, the shorter the angle of vision becomes and the more the framework of action becomes constricted to smaller and smaller time sequences.

Of course, at the level of particular human beings the principle of discursivity was instituted quite some time ago with the invention of the autonomous individual, and in a way the larger cycles of reciprocity we see in political contexts are simply an expansion of the principles of autonomy. Here is where the discursive is seen at its most ironic, though, for— as Hegel's master/slave dialectic shows once again—the individual can only demonstrate his individuality through the assertion of power over another, yet to do so is to deny the principle of individuality, for it establishes a reciprocal network of relations. Individuality is thus denied through the assertion of it, and this too reinforces the spirit of revenge because it makes clear that the individual is dependent on another at the same time that it necessitates a denial of the fact. Every cycle of reciprocation must be based on a displacement of the knowledge of reciprocity, and every displacement causes the reciprocation to return with still more force.

The power of these reciprocal networks was certainly not invented by discursive practice itself; it is a human force that antedates any modern practices, though contemporary humans have put it most emphatically to use. Indeed, if there is a chief value to discursivity, it is that it has so expanded the forces of reciprocation that it becomes increasingly hard to ignore them. In this way, the heart of the problem was reached with the invention of the individual, for only conferring an autonomous and independent power on everyone could conceivably lead to the understanding that individuality and autonomy were possible for no one. Only by extending the principle of autonomy to everything could we begin thoroughly to demonstrate the interrelations that nothing could escape. As long as there were readily available locations of exclusion that would accept their exclusiveness, belief in autonomy was still possible, for reciprocity could be denied by imagining a world where the excluded were dependent but the included were not. Only when the master is forced to deny his autonomy from the slave is it possible to see how the reciprocal forces work; even more important, only when the slave has the power to become the master can he see that the master too is enslaved to the principle of reciprocity. Until that moment arises, the slave can always imagine the master as immune from the dependency of resentment that he so strenuously feels. The great virtue of discursive practice is that it made possible for the first time the full dissemination of this principle and the understanding of it. That it did so through a denial of it is less important than that it made its force visible to everyone in its attempt forever to displace it onto the excluded whose function it always was to bear this burden. The purpose of the excluded is to embody those categories that man does not want to face within himself— not only to define the limit of the appropriately human but more importantly to deny that the human always extends farther than we are willing to admit. And as Foucault's work demonstrates, the profusion of categories of exclusion—and their increasing solidification through institutionalization— shows more and more evidently those aspects of the human that man does not want to face and demonstrates that man is finding it increasingly hard to avoid facing those aspects of himself he has always tried to deny.

The difficulty in breaking through the vicious circle of revenge and its revulsion against time is thus in one sense increased by our need more and more strenuously to deny its presence, but the extension of this principle to every domain also makes its denial increasingly more difficult. If one cannot find any particular place to break through the circle to show its logic and the effects that it has, then at least one can hope that the extension of its powers to every domain will ultimately make it impossible to avoid or deny.

Even if we were to imagine such an event happening, though, as both Nietzsche and Heidegger did, we would still have to face the dilemmas it presents to us. If the power of the discursive was based on modes of exclusion that are inherent in the nature of the questions we raised—as the unconcealed/concealed perspective would suggest—it is not enough to recognize that the power of discursivity came about through the assertion of exclusion at the same time that it denied the consequences of its exclusivity. To recognize that this double bind is at the heart of discursive practice is to have confronted that which we have chosen to ignore, but it still leaves us with the problem of how to deal with the recursive differences we have learned to accept. If all questions are unconcealings that also conceal; if all illumination is obtained only by the darkness that enframes it; if, in short, recursive practice is inherently inclusive and exclusive at the same time, how are we to find our way out of the dilemmas our own activities are based on? How can we avoid the exclusionary principle at the heart of any mode of questioning, at the heart of any mode of order?

The most obvious point to make—though it is by no means sufficient in itself—is that recursive practice begins with an awareness of difference and a knowledge of the way it works. Given this, it acknowledges the repressive dangers inherent in the question and thus seeks to account for them from the beginning. Furthermore, recursive practice is based on the lack of ground for difference; inasmuch as all differences are contextually based, that which they bring to light is always partially qualified by the context through which the question takes place. Without a ground for the differences—and without a desire for one—there is no attempt to institutionalize particular differences in order to establish the power of the question. The recursive derives its power from always being on the way, from always recognizing the need to turn back to explore that which was left hidden in the original opening. Because of this, it works against the grain of the recursive to stop the flow of questions or to attempt to base them on a ground that will allow them to become static and repressive in their delimitations of what is included and excluded.

In accepting difference, the recursive also has a different attitude toward it, for the difference that defines the question is not centered on the need to deny the connection to the other side of the difference. It accepts the reciprocal nature of definition inherent in difference and does not seek to establish the priority of one side over the other. To do so would be to hide what the recursive can reveal by its return upon itself. The recursive difference, in other words, establishes its values not by asserting the priority of one aspect over another but rather by establishing the essential interconnectedness of the two that makes the value of one aspect inconceivable without equal attention to its other aspect. There is, to be sure, no guarantee that one will construe the value of difference in this way, but then there is no guarantee within discursive practice that the implementation of difference will be put to good use either, and the odds are greater for misuse in discursive practice because it is always based on the belief of separable, autonomous values that can assert priority over the differences.

To specify a bit more what is at stake here, I should like to suggest the example that Foucault began with in his discussion of the birth of the insane asylum. The traditional way of looking at the matter would be to say that the asylum was instituted seriously in the eighteenth century—and insanity along with it—because society came to identify a certain segment of itself as sufficiently different to threaten it. Thus, whereas people with various kinds of mental differences were previously allowed more or less to be present within the social network so long as they found ways of sustaining themselves that did not threaten the social order, they all came to be seen as a category that had to be excluded from society in order to maintain order. The invention of insanity thus shed a different kind of light on that segment of society; insanity as a defining characteristic, if you will, "unconcealed" something about a group of people that came to define these individuals and to delimit their role in society in a different way. And sometimes the motives for exclusion of the mad could even have been construed as good—people sought to incarcerate them "for their own good" in order to make sure that they were properly attended to. The discursive mode at its best would seek to unravel the complexity of motivation developed through this new institution, but basically it would restrict its analysis to an elaboration in some fashion of the points I have mentioned here.

Foucault, however, would address himself to the concealed aspect of this exchange; he would investigate the relationship between that which has been excluded and that which was included as a result. He would turn to what purposes it served for the sane to invent the insane and would pursue the changes in the definition of sanity that were produced as a result of the exclusion of the mad. He would seek what powers were gained by those who came to define their sanity and their power through the exclusion inherent in the definition of the insane. The emergence of the difference works both ways, and indeed, it works more importantly in the direction Foucault pursues, for those who established the difference had the most to gain by it just as they had the most to gain by denying any essential connection between their power and the network of relations they established through delimiting the category of the insane. When it becomes clear that the institution of reason as the guiding force in the world was achieved in part through the implementation of the category of the insane, then we begin to see what is at issue here, for again, reason itself is devoted to the principle that its activities are value-free and that they are based on the law of noncontradiction—as such, reason obtains its force both by establishing the insane and by denying any real connection to that category of human behavior. What is at stake is not the awareness of difference itself, for differences were readily apparent before the development of the asylum; what is at stake is the network of power that is built up out of the establishment of the asylum and the denial of its connection to reason. Differences were established in this context because someone had something to gain by them, yet the emergence of reason and those who profited from its emergence remain hidden in traditional discourse. The assertion of difference and the denial of the interrelatedness inherent in it allow the displacement of the problem to occur while the gains of the included are institutionalized, and the desire to institutionalize the difference without conceding its full ramifications leads to the forgetfulness about this historical moment.

The same principle is most obviously at work today in the context of minorities and women, for no matter how strenuously difference is denied in both cases, it is also most apparent. A woman announces her difference by being female, and a black announces his difference by not being white. In possessing such clear differences, these excluded humans face almost insuperable obstacles, for the differences cannot be denied. One who profits from the established value judgment of the male/female or black/white difference can concede the essential humanness of both categories because the values inherent in the difference are so solidified that nothing is lost by asserting the humanness. The values and power of "man" have so saturated the cultural network—and the definition of "man" is so dependent on the exclusion of "female"—that a simple assertion of similitude makes no difference and costs nothing. The balance is not redressed or even seriously addressed because the values presently constituted through the difference are denied and the position thus seemingly put out of play. And at this point only the denial of difference allows the value system to remain in place because to accept the difference is to be forced to reconsider the values presently embodied in it.

In this case the women's movement has done its best to unconceal that which was hidden in the establishment of difference, so the network of relations and the stakes involved are somewhat clearer, yet at the same time in large part the ironic effect of this illumination has been the reinforcement of the values inherent in it. The values in the male/female or black/white difference were not simply the denial of status, means, and power to women or blacks; nor were they simply the assertion of male and white power over women and blacks and the fruits that ensued from their exclusion. More importantly, the values and power embodied in the distinction were that power is achieved through this exclusionary principle and the denial of its implementation—women and blacks are like the insane in this respect, for they are simply two more categories through which this process has been implemented and extended. And whereas that is a serious problem in its own right, the more problematic issue is the definition of "male" that is embodied in the general practice of which these are only specific examples. Even though it may be true that one can only confront the general practice by using it against itself, at the same time it is clear that the greater part of the women's movement has lost sight of the values of the general practice—instead of embodying a critique of the values inherent in "man," the movement seems more interested in appropriating them, thereby losing sight of the more fundamental issue and simply, in effect, arguing that women too have the right to abuse the principle of difference through exclusionary practices that simply put them on the "right" side of the equation. Not only is the battle not being won, the war seems to have been lost altogether, much as though the process itself invites human forgetfulness at the earliest possible moment.

I have used these examples simply because they are most compelling in our own historical context and also because they show the forgetfulness that is an institutionalized part of the problem. In the more obvious relations of power, though, the principle is never really forgotten—it is simply not spoken about. Kings, for example, doubtless knew of the complicity of their power and the grounds upon which it always stood. It might have been the case that the king/subject relationship had a tendency in normal circumstances to reveal the king's role while the subject's remained hidden, just as in normal times it was the king's power and presumed autonomy from the subject that seemed essential, either because of historical practice or as a result of some notion of divine right. But the king knew—and the subjects could be easily reminded—that his power derived from his subjects and that they could assert their power over him if they saw fit to do so. The relationship could be denied as if magically to eliminate it, but the denial was always a magical one, and the king simply had to trace the narrow threshold between denial and awareness just as any modern leader today does.

The attitude toward difference must thus begin by a reconsideration of the values embodied in the present system of differences, moving both ways across the threshold that divides and holds them together. Equally, the attitude toward difference cannot forget that the threshold divides *and* ties together, for otherwise only a new series of differences will emerge upon the old exclusionary principles. Man must be double-sighted if he is to avoid forgetting what he leaves behind when he turns his eyes. The attitude toward difference must finally be based on the notion that values emerge from difference but that the difference cannot ever definitively establish the value of one side over another without denying their integral relationship.

The difference without ground, however, raises questions about the larger social network and the institutions through which it constitutes itself. We have traditionally seen the virtue of social networks precisely in their ability to establish a ground upon which activity can be based, and if the recursive has no ground, it seems to undermine the security upon which humans depend and for which they construct social systems in the first place. It is possible to imagine institutions without grounds, but how are we to conceive of them in practical contexts? If we cannot imagine the implementation of such a system, then we seem to be in dire straits indeed, for the only two other readily available possibilities are to accept the inherent abusiveness of our networks of exclusion and simply fight for our position among the elect, or to move toward some kind of radical decentralization of institutions that would seek to overcome their power by cutting them down to a more human scale. The former position obviously fails to eliminate any of the basic problems of our present networks, and the latter seems to raise incredible practical and logistical problems that seem equally insuperable.

Even if radical decentralization were a positive goal, the question of its implementation creates its own problems. Structurally speaking, it took a long time for the institutions we have to develop their present size, and in large part that length of time was necessary to accommodate the changes they introduced; any abrupt reversal of the process would entail great shocks and cause chaos in the modes of distribution that have allowed the earth to sustain the human population that it presently contains. The dissolution of these networks would be far more repressive than their continuation, at least in the short run, and in the long run would be sustainable only if large numbers of humans were eliminated. Pragmatically speaking, decentralization on a large scale seems not to be a viable option at the moment.

The larger question is whether decentralization is consistent with the possibilities of recursivity, whether it works with it or against its grain. To the extent that decentralization means a loosening of the network of exclusionary principles through which our present system operates, it certainly works out of recursivity, for it is designed to deny proprietary rights to those who established the grounds of the institutions and thus might go some way toward reversing the values of difference. But radical decentralization—as expressed through Gilles Deleuze's concept of the nomad, for example—seems to deny the interconnectedness of difference by seeking to minimize the number of possible differences that are inscribed in any particular network. The nomad as symbol suggests our return to the individual whose only major shift is against the concept of property rights. The value of the nomad stems from his always being on the way and from his living a life wholly consistent with that lack of ground, and as such it presents a viable alternative—but the nomad also achieves that life by severely limiting the possibilities in his social network. If we are to profit from him, we must somehow be able to establish his loose social network and his on-the-wayness within the larger collectivity we have come to repre-

sent, and that can only be done through a process of decentralization that does not dissolve everything but merely un-
grounds that which forms the base from which we make our
choices.

In order for difference not to be repressive, in order for it
to avoid the aggressive implementation of difference against
itself, difference must come to be free-floating—differences
need to be seen as part of an endless flow rather than as
irreducible and static modes of social evaluation. Institutions
must have sites—they cannot avoid having them—but the
sites cannot be fixed, nor can our conception of their functions
be static. This means first of all that we must recognize that
repression itself is the arbitrary imposition of difference that
denies the reciprocal flow across the threshold while still
making use of that flow, and second that we must come to
see the productivity of difference in terms of sustaining the
play of difference rather than in terms of establishing a domi-
nance/subordination equation that attempts to freeze the system of relations once and for all. It is not that we are even
capable of freezing the relations, as the master/slave dialectic
shows; it is rather once again a question of the attitude we
bring to the dialectic itself. A differential equation is an equation of difference, and its value derives from that.

The repression involved in difference is the result not only
of the desire to establish dominance; more importantly it is a
denial of time itself—through time, the differences flow back
and forth across the threshold of their difference, and one
who seeks to establish them in a static relationship desires to
negate time. For only by negating time can the represser avoid
confronting the fact that all differences eventually return, that
the desire for revenge that led to the institutionalization of the
difference will ultimately displace the values so imposed—the
network of difference continues to oscillate in spite of one's
attempt to stop it, so only by denying time can one lead
oneself to believe that one has conquered the flow of difference. Repression thus involves the use of difference while
denying the necessity of its laws; it is a short-term solution
for one's revulsion against time that in the long term imposes
the greater necessity of accepting the force of time from a

vantage point of weakness rather than strength. The inevitability of this logic nevertheless too frequently manages to be ignored, and it is perhaps the greatest tragedy of human events that people can so easily deny that which can never be overcome in the long run. The motives for ignorance might always be strong, but the incentives for understanding are, or at least should be, always stronger.

If we are to imagine a world in which the difference of difference is allowed to be what it is, we must also be capable of understanding the inevitable, for the difference of difference can never be indefinitely deferred, and the attempt so to defer it only continues man's backward regression away from understanding. It is as though man has always been fighting a guerrilla war that he must always ultimately lose, yet he keeps up the battle because he knows of nothing else he can do. Any species that could devote more than two thousand years to the dream of identity without seeing the consequences or the futility of the dream has a powerful need to deny the real. One is forced to conclude that man has used his thought against himself for millennia, so his need to deny the difference of difference must be so compelling that even his best instruments of understanding are employed to avoid knowledge, to turn away from the only truth that can never be denied. When Freud talked about this impulse in terms of the death instinct, he made sure to qualify his every move by stating and restating that he was only speculating, that he had no empirical evidence for his ideas, that it was rather a lack of empirical evidence to explain the repetition compulsion that led him to his conception in the first place. There was, in short, a difference within the repetition compulsion that could not be adequately explained according to conventional theories of interpretation, and it was to fill this void that Freud imagined the death instinct. And not only does he show that he is apologetic for having to do so, he also clearly wishes that such speculation were not necessary—he would very much have liked to explain everything in terms of the life instinct and the pleasure principle, but he had the courage to recognize what we always choose to avoid, the death instinct that dominates our desire to deny difference and to deny our revulsion against time. The emergence of the death instinct in Freud's work comes cautiously, regretfully, then, but when it does finally appear it can no longer be avoided any more than Nietzsche's thought of the eternal return can. They can be deferred, displaced, and derided, but they cannot be ignored.

It is possible that all great civilizations construct themselves on the denial of the difference of difference and that all of the fruits of their toil come from this denial. And if this is true, then it would seem to follow that the unavoidable emergence of the difference of difference would mark the beginning of the end for the power of that civilization. Nietzsche, Freud, and Heidegger would thus come to mark the decline of Western civilization, a slide that accelerates with the growing awareness of the inevitability of the difference of difference. If man's power to transform the earth necessarily derives from his death instinct and from the equally necessary choice to deny it, then we must indeed conclude that our cultures are headed toward decay. At the very least one would have to believe in this necessity if one were to continue to deny the force of the difference of difference in the face of its now-overwhelming evidence. We do not merely have to speculate about its presence any more, for it has been made all too obvious. The only way around it is to continue furiously to deny it in the hope that that will keep the embers burning a while longer. The difference of difference is unavoidable, even if ignorance of it is not.

If Western cultures have built themselves upon a denial of difference, though, it by no means follows that human societies must necessarily be constructed on this ground. One could argue that it is inevitable that man performs great feats only through the revenge that seeks to deny yet always confirms his revulsion against time, but that would indeed be a speculative principle, for we have no evidence of that necessity within our own history to confirm it. That we have no evidence is certainly strong testimony about the power of the death instinct, but it says nothing about the intrinsic strength of the life instinct as it is brought into place against our impulses of denial, unless the traditional dominance of the death instinct over the life instinct implies that it is a greater force. But this is obviously not the case in the larger sphere of activity, for life is very obviously still present in spite of the force of our repetition compulsion to negate it.

If we are to imagine a culture that derives its greatness from accepting the differential aspect inherent in the life instinct/ death instinct difference rather than denying their reciprocal relations, where would we turn first for evidence? We could investigate those situations where we have come to see that things have taken on a "life of their own," for the contexts in which we use that expression suggest both our surprise that things have indeed taken on a life of their own—that is, our human intervention seems not to work in spite of our attempts to impose it—and also our sense that things have gotten out of control, that we must submit to their force rather than deny it. The irony inherent in the general use of the expression "taking on a life of its own" is that it suggests that it is indeed life that has taken over, but that we clearly wish it had not. This would not necessarily imply that we would have pre-ferred death to have taken over, but it might suggest that our attempts to impose the force of our death instinct upon the situation have failed, which would imply that we wanted the death instinct to take over.

Whatever the specific relation between the two impulses might be in such cases, they do clearly reveal our dismay at our lack of control. As with most denials of difference, when such situations occur our tendency is to see only one thing revealed—our lack of control—without perceiving the recip-rocal connections between that lack of control and the life that is going on in spite of it. The vectors of investigation only point to one part of the differential relation: "Things have taken on a life of their own/we have lost control" is an ac-knowledged difference, but it is conceded only so we may seek to reassert our will. We only investigate our modes of control and how they can be reestablished, and while our attempts to reassert control might force us to question what it is about that life of its own that has made it a life of its own, we are not really interested in its life, only in control over it, so our understanding ultimately reinforces our knowledge of control without contributing greatly to our knowledge of the life that we seek to subdue.

The more fruitful investigation would pursue the reasons why the process has taken on a life of its own, how this life limits our control, and what those limits say about life and about our control. We turn away from such queries because things frighten us when they take on a life of their own, so our procedures are always carried out under the guise of crisis management. And inasmuch as crisis management is that human procedure whereby we seek to investigate the local causes of the problem in order to attend to them and resolve the crisis, we lose sight of the relationship between the local causes and the larger life of its own. Once things have been patched together and the local causes identified, we then address them in order to prevent things from repeating themselves. This done, the crisis-management team disbands, confident that it has reestablished control and equally convinced that it has learned something in the process because in identifying the local cause and correcting it, it thinks it has learned how to prevent such incidents from occurring again in the future.

And indeed, something is learned about the local causes in these procedures, just as something is grasped about the nature of crisis management, and those are valuable gains. What is not discerned, though, is the relation of those local changes to the larger field of which they are a part; what is equally not learned or even investigated is the nature and process of things taking on a life of their own and what that means for man's understanding, to say nothing for his control. The results of these procedures in any historical epoch are that the crucial things are never learned; we obtain specific understanding without learning anything about life or control. If the world thus comes to look like a pipe that is always bursting in one place or another, we can at the very least argue that we have become more adept at patching the holes when they occur, as we know they inevitably will, even if we treat each hole as a nonrepeatable event in the hope that it will not repeat itself.

We need then to look at the relationship between local

causes in these circumstances and try to discern what they can tell us about the life that will always inevitably take over from our control. The example that comes most readily to mind is our institutions, each in its own way set up at the command of man in accord with the implementation of a specific difference, or rectification of difference; each in turn seemingly inevitably multiplying its functions and constituencies to the point where it takes on a life of its own and no longer seems to respond adequately to our control. One could argue that the basic problem is our tendency always to want to extend our understanding or control over more and more terrain; more cynically this could be construed as the simple desire for power. According to this scenario, the institution grows in little steps at first, then more rapidly, and finally by geometrical leaps and bounds, all because the individuals who want power invent functions and constituencies to place under their control, and the people who serve these functions and constituencies in turn invent their own, and so on until control no longer seems possible. In this view, to control the impulse to power would prevent the institution from getting out of control, yet this is precisely what humans seem to lack. The problem is aggravated further because we have no idea at what point in such systems things actually begin to get out of control. As with a nuclear weapon, the system seems to have a critical mass, below which the maintenance of order can be achieved, above which control rapidly disappears. Because we focus on local causes rather than on larger series of events, we know very little about critical masses of this kind; we only know that when they arrive they are very difficult to reverse, much as a violent mob is hard to diffuse once it has had a chance to emerge with full force.

Another, more general view of the situation would suggest that while impulses like man's desire for power might contribute to the metastasization of institutions, the problem is really rooted more in the nature of networks themselves. Institutions generally begin with a relatively specific set of functions and are manageable within that framework, but in implementing its functions, the institution necessarily grows in complexity. Functions are implemented with respect to some group or other, but they inevitably generate responses, many of which were unforeseen. Those in charge seek to address the unforeseen responses and thus make the functions more specific, or else broader, depending on the context. As further implementation proceeds, the "machine" needs to be fine tuned more and more or given a bigger engine or have its major components redefined. Each of these moves in itself may be clearly defined and perfectly justifiable, but the total effect is a network of functions that is no longer understandable, and one that seeks further to expand its complexity of response. In this sense, institutions are simply like other organisms, and their activities emerge over a larger and larger terrain as a matter of course as long as they are not checked by some other institution or function. Again, there is a critical mass of complexity and reproduction at which the functions of an institution do actually take on a life of their own outside of our control, and when this happens we are all too powerless to attend to the matter because we do not even know how these difficulties come about.

Within this model, two key points can be identified, the first of which is our lack of understanding of the critical mass, the second of which is our general lack of understanding of complex networks. We tend either to study things in isolation or in aggregates, and neither of those modes works when it comes to the emergence and growth of complex systems. We do talk about "young" bureaucracies and "senile" ones, suggesting their lifelike qualities, but we know relatively little about their life processes. We do know, however, that one of their most striking features is that they are deliberately grounded, and because they cannot move on but only build outward from a center, they already bear a strange lack of resemblance to other creatures, all of whom are grounded at best on the earth, otherwise remaining mobile within various noncentered fields. If the complex network of the jackrabbit population grows to a point where it takes on a life of its own, the profusion of life will be held in check because the jackrabbit is not the center of its domain, because there is no center in its domain, because the fields of force are multiple and constantly shifting, and the multiplicity of fields and their shifts in most cases is sufficient in itself to hold the profusion in check. Because institutions seek so strenuously to be grounded, though, the movement that would keep their forces in check is curtailed; indeed, the ground itself is so unnatural that it too has a tendency to redistribute the forces in perverse ways.

It is not that man and his institutions are the sole functions in our world that have no predators to keep them in check, as some people would argue. Humans capitulate to the same forces the jackrabbit does, only less obviously because we cannot readily observe those forces. Nor are these forces that control us always readily apparent: the ability to produce and disseminate food, the limits of human physiology, and so forth. We tend to attribute demographic changes to circumstances like this, and to social, economic, and historical developments, but there are also powerful natural checking mechanisms. Pollution is the most obvious one, but climatic and other such changes also play a part, to say nothing for the more complex variables involved. We tend to think, for example, that "stress-related" diseases are simple responses to a complex and changing world, which they are, but surely they are equally checks on the system that generated them, and many of them are as unknown as the mysterious word *stress* suggests, covering as it does our ignorance. These checks are much more present than our studies show, for we only investigate the louder voices. We know, for example, that the average American male produces only about half as many sperm per ejaculation as he did forty years ago, and we know that if this trend continues more than half the male population will be sterile within fifty years, but we do not know exactly why this is happening. We attribute the change to chemicals in the environment and to stress, and they may well have something to do with the problem. But the one thing that is certain is that this shift is not accidental; it is a response to our actions within the world and is a checking mechanism as powerful as any larger predator would be.

It would seem that any network, as part of a series of networks, is inevitably submitted to checks on its force all the time, and this is as true for institutions as it is for the physical production of humans. The problem is that we do not look for such checks, and as a result we have not begun to investigate them. Life is held in check because it has a life of its own, over which no particular species has control, but it is also held in check because of the built-in parameters of response to life in the fields within which it occurs. It is a very old story that most species manage to mark the limits of their terrain and power with a limited amount of death; we know equally that within the average species the same process occurs without usually leading to a fight to the death. But we pride ourselves on the fact that we are different from other species in this regard, even though we are not. We may indeed kill each other with fairly reckless abandon, but in general we test the limits of our power in knowing and nonviolent ways. Yet short of the more obvious studies on how these processes work through gesture and space—identification of parts but not the larger processes—we have failed to see how life, having a life of its own, develops and checks its profusion in predictable ways. We know of the processes but ignore them all the same. We have become, in short, adept at identification, but we fail as a matter of course to understand what we have identified.

Likewise, because we fail to understand life as it takes on a life of its own, and because we are frightened when we become aware that it always *does* have a life of its own, our fear prevents us from learning anything about the process or about the context through which it manifests itself. If an institution has taken on a life of its own, it is probably being more effective in some ways than when it was seemingly under our control—it might tell us how the institution could better serve the purposes for which it was designed, or it might even show us what was wrong with the purposes for which it was designed and how we could redevelop our understanding of the field through which the institution works and so put to use the life that it has allowed to emerge. We make no such inquiries because our fear overrides our desire to understand and because we think we already know the lessons that can be learned from the situation. And once again it is the lesson of the master/slave dialectic. We "know" that when institutions grow too large we no longer co͏͏ them—they control us; we thus "know" that bigness is ͏͏ enemy we must face, even if with great difficulty. In "know ing" these things, and in having identified the problem as "bigness," we think we have resolved the difficulty. We have simply conferred too much power on the slave, and having done so, we find that the slave now has power over us. But bigness is not the problem at all—after all, the same process occurs on equally minute levels like the cancer cell. We assume that institutions, like humans, are driven by a revulsion against time and so seek to be the master that can deny it. This would make perfect sense inasmuch as we are ourselves busily denying the existence of these principles while we try to put them to use.

What we come to understand when we look at the institution that takes on a life of its own is what we have been discovering ever since the shift from Newton to Einstein took place—that the world does not so much resemble a structure as it does a system, if by structure we mean a static framework that contains the world and by system we mean an interlocking set of networks that is constantly changing. The structural, spatial metaphor was much more congenial to the value-free world we sought to establish through our institutions, but the systemic view seems more appropriate to the world in which we now live. The structure is that over against which life asserts itself, and the system is that which sees life as taking on a life of its own, in which we participate, and against which we can rebel, but over which we can have no final and definitive control. Thus, our institutions resist structure and assert system's priority over structure—we may have systems management and systems analysis and the like, but we still resist the tendency to think in terms of systems just as we fail to see our institutions as the systems they are. We have learned to talk about systems without actually seeing in terms of them. And if we were to look at those bureaucracies that have taken on a life of their own, the first thing we would see is that they have done so because they are essentially systems rather than structures. We then might notice that they do not really have a life of their own—they only have a life that does not fully and appropriately respond to our commands. We can affect their lives, but not as we think we ought to be able to; instead, they are affected more pertinently by the other networks within which they work, some of which we established, some of which have always been beyond our control. The problem in failing to see this is that we do have some control over them, but it gets imposed in the most perverse of ways. Institutions, like other systems, are always susceptible to abuse in any case, and the possibilities of misuse only increase when we lose control of them, for we are then no longer certain of exactly what functions they are to serve—lacking this understanding, the possibility of local causes asserting themselves over the larger concerns of the network increases, and we then begin to diagnose the disease of the institution in terms of the abuses that simply increased as a result of our failure to understand our own invention.

If we are to face these problems, and the more basic question of the difference of difference out of which they arise, we must turn our attention toward the systems of life and the ways that they take on lives of their own so that we can properly take our place within them rather than resisting their power. This does not mean that we need to abandon institutions or even necessarily that we must cut them down to size. It does mean that we need to investigate their principles in order to understand how best to make use of them, something we certainly have not done up to this point. As a matter of convenience, one place to begin this investigation would be on the other side of those things that take on a life of their own, for there are many cases where we use that phrase with wonder rather than fear. Sometimes novelists are given to saying that their fiction after a certain point clearly takes on a life of its own, after which the writer himself feels bound to accept certain kinds of inevitability. Once character and plot have been set in motion and allowed to develop to a certain point, they seem to be dictating to the author what he can and cannot do with them. It is not that he is no longer able to make choices, but rather that his choices are more limited if he is to respond properly to the ones he has already made. He can always reject the life of its own the novel has taken on and go with the plot or the character where he wants to, but the result is generally less than satisfactory. So the novelist finds his choices being shaped by that which he has already written, and this is usually a good sign, for it suggests that he has given his novel enough complexity and interrelatedness to let it take its own path. And while specific choices are still open, they must now respond to the texture of what is already given, limiting the possibilities in one sense, but in another sense confirming the value of the choices that have already been made.

The fiction's difference from the author asserts itself, and the writing becomes a dialectic in which the author must participate if he is not to go against the difference of the text. This could be seen as a form of bondage rather than simple discipline, but it makes better sense to see it as a form of discipline, for it has great benefits for the writer. Most pertinently, the novel takes the author where he cannot go without it—he establishes the context for the action, he frames the general nature of the characters, and he does so largely on the basis of what he knows about character and situation. But when these things take on a life of their own, when they establish their difference from the author—for the author only begins to recognize the power of the text when it suggest another choice than his, thus asserting its difference—then the text begins to take him into the unknown. It begins to teach him about the effects of the complexities of plot and character and invites him to learn about the effects of his own decisions. If the characters take on a life of their own, they have the power to reveal what it is like when things do take on a life of their own, and they also have to power to probe farther into character itself than the author is capable of on his own. The characters come to know more about character than the novelist does, so he must now learn from them.

Of course, in many respects the novel always had a life of its own, and when the author reaches the point where he confirms the parameters of inevitability within it, he is merely coming to be aware of what was there from the beginning. For the inevitabilities are not simply based on the complexities introduced that wish to move in certain directions. They are also located in the choice of form, which has in one way dictated the procedures from the outset, even though we are wont to say that the author chose to write a novel. In large part, the novel chose to write him when he saw that it was the form that was appropriate to what he wanted to accomplish. In choosing him, the form has had a life of its own from the beginning, so when the author comes to see inevitability creeping in, he is confirming the power of the form at the same time that he is expanding the possibilities inherent in it. Likewise, the subject matter of the novel chose the writer as much as he chose it. It may be based on his own experiences, but he has doubtless had a great many experiences, and not all of them called out to receive fictional treatment. And when one includes various other historical and social contingencies, to which the author is equally responding, we can see how many of the choices have been made for him from the outset. His particular context brings all these contingencies together, and it gives these contingencies the opportunity to develop into something different, but they have had a large part in the choosing even before the novel was conceived.

When the novelist confronts the moment when his text is clearly speaking with a voice of its own, he is simply allowing it to confirm that the value of his work is in large part derived from his willingness to respond to its difference. He thus begins to see how the creative force of his fiction is a result of similar kinds of acceptance along the way. He may have chosen it simply because it seemed compelling to him, but when he accepts the difference of the novel he is also beginning to see what was really compelling in the incident he chose—he is learning what was right about the situation that seemed right to him when he chose it. The author is not moving blindly from a past he knows little about into a future he knows even less about; rather, he is moving out of a past that he has accepted, and he is finding out what kind of past has chosen him. In learning about the past that has chosen him, he is also inquiring into the future that emerges from the past that is already given. Far from being blind, then, his vision moves with greater certainty because he has accepted the past that has chosen him. Seen in this light, the moment of inevitability in the novelist's work is that point when he must consciously choose either fully to accept or reject his own past. He is not simply making a choice about the course of his novel, for if that were true there would be no real inevitability involved in its difference. Instead, the inevitability casts light on the past out of which this difference emerged, and he cannot deny the inevitability of his novel without negating his past as well.

A similar kind of inevitability is found in that moment when Freud approached the death instinct. His inquiries had led him to the point where they had their own inevitability, and what they told him was that his speculations were insufficient, that if what he had already written was true, there was more to be said, that the death instinct was a necessary part of his speculation. Freud does not really want to concede the death instinct, for it runs counter to his ideas about psychology and life; but if he rejects it, he not only denies the value of his work and its inevitability, he also denies his past, out of which the inevitability originally arose. His very tentative movements in *Beyond the Pleasure Principle* are thus not simply the result of a lack of empirical evidence for his proposition, nor are they the result of his distaste for the death instinct's creeping into the center of life—the tentativeness is a mark of the stake in his past and his acceptance of it, and thus in turn a reflection of his stake in his future that is based on the acceptance of his past. In one sense, as is the case with any writer who faces this moment, it would have been easier for Freud to turn away from the death instinct, for if the pleasure principle could not adequately account for everything that was involved in the repetition compulsion, there was no necessary reason why some day a way might not be found for it fully to account for the compulsion. And inasmuch as Freud himself was the only one who knew how assiduously he had tried to accommodate the repetition compulsion to the pleasure principle; inasmuch as only he knew how completely this failed to account for the phenomena he had observed; he could have rejected the death instinct as a possibility, either leaving it to others to uncover it or hoping that someone else would be able to accommodate the repetition compulsion to the pleasure principle. Nor would anyone have known that Freud would have rejected his past in doing so.

These moments of inevitability—in novelists or psychoanalysts or anyone else—are tests of the strength of man, for they demand the acceptance of difference that allows one to accede to one's past, and that is no minor challenge. Perhaps there are so few significant writers because hardly any of them are willing to accept the inevitability of this moment and all it involves, in which case part of the value of the writer's work is that it shows us how we must accept the inevitability and in turn shows us the results of embracing it. To accede to the "It was" in the moment of inevitability is to grant the difference of difference, and only by accepting it can the truly significant arise. It may be true that many writers develop their work out of their sense of revulsion for the "It was"— Flaubert is a good example—but in doing so they are also having to accept its inevitability in one way or another, at least for the moment; they are forced to accept their own past in order to be able to confront their revulsion toward it.

When a novel takes on a life of its own, we might say that the author has lost control, but his control was never as strong as we like to think it is anyway. When a novel takes on a life of its own, the novelist is merely conceding that his own life has a life of its own as much as the novel does, and that only in embracing *that* life has he been able to arrive at the point where he can accept the "It was" that is part of his life's life of its own. In confronting this moment, the novelist comes to see that his strength and his creative force have always come from accepting that his life has a life of its own—only because he is willing to be led by it has he been able to arrive at the point where he can accept that he *has* been led by it. The spur and growth of his own development as a human being and as a novelist have come from his acceptance of this inevitability even if it begins as a struggle against it. Indeed, the struggles against the inevitability are an essential aspect of confirming one's life as having a life of its own, and in part the struggle is that which most fruitfully allows the life to emerge. But the struggle against the inevitability has its value embodied in accepting the inevitability, for once it is cut loose from those moorings, the death instinct takes over.

It goes without saying that the manner in which things take on a life of their own runs counter to much of what we like to think and once again raises all those problems about the emergence of the inimical in the world. Acceptance of the inevitability that life takes on a life of its own is seen as capitulation to the flux, as giving up one's responsibility for one's actions, as blindly giving oneself over to any possibility and as the abandonment of all values. The arguments against accepting the inevitability are well known and well rehearsed, as they ought to be inasmuch as they have predominated in our thought since Plato's time. Against these charges, one can only respond as I have throughout. One can argue that far from being the denial of values, the acceptance of inevitability makes values possible in the first place. One can argue that acceptance of inevitability does not mean capitulation to the flux any more than it means that one accepts everything as inevitable—what one accepts as inevitable is simply that life takes on a life of its own, but this is far from suggesting that one must capitulate to everything. Nor does it mean that once one has accepted the inevitable one is finished with his task, for the inevitability of the inevitable must always be questioned—otherwise one has no way of knowing what can and cannot be changed. Likewise, the acceptance of inevitability does not mean that one is powerless in the face of one's past and future alike. The inevitability emerges through our productive actions within life—we participate in the inevitability we allow to emerge and give it its color and shape just as we give man the color and shape he has through the manner in which we allow the inevitabilities of which he is a part to emerge. Accepting the inevitable does not mean that the world is a deterministic place where humans are mere automatons; on the contrary, it means that man is that much less of an automaton to the extent that he accepts the inevitability that is always part of his actions. Without this acceptance, man merely repeats the revenge and the revulsion against time that generates revenge in the first place. One's possibilities thus open up through an acceptance of inevitability and a regular questioning of it rather than closing down and reducing man to a creature whose choices are at best limited to the insignificant and at worst open to little more than ceaseless acts of revenge. One makes one's future by accepting the "It was" out of which it will necessarily emerge even as one makes one's own future possible by the same acceptance. Contrary to the horrific scenarios that are conjured up when the inevitability presents itself, the horrific scenarios can only be avoided if man accepts the inevitability and works from there.

Perhaps the values involved in this most crucial of choices can be better seen in a situation where we can more carefully explore the inevitability of something's taking on a life of its own that has a clearly identifiable past to it that we can investigate, and there is no better site for this than the history of scientific inquiry itself. The most significant point in the history of science, short of its "inception," was again the moment when its line of inquiry led it to reject the Newtonian model of the universe for the Einsteinian one. Up to that point, though there were shifts and ruptures in its mode of questioning, it was still possible to base the shifts in thought on the mechanical model of the universe—in this sense, up to the shift away from Newton, science appeared much like a novel that was inevitably writing itself. Scientists formulated the questions and the experiments, but the assumption was that those queries were helping to unfold the "plot" and "character" of the universe. This line of inquiry was much more deterministic than the mode that followed, and the inevitabilities inherent in it were stronger as well.

As I have argued earlier, when the shift between Newton and Einstein took place, there was always the possibility that scientists could refuse to accept it, just as Einstein was unwilling to accept the full consequences of quantum theory. Man's desire to know was offset by the fact that so much of the novel of the world already seemed to be written—although it is true that Newtonian theory was not abandoned, only modified and thus improved—this way of looking at the shift fails to point out sufficiently the force of changing the central metaphor of the enterprise and the need to reconstruct the plot on the basis of the new metaphor. The shift dictated a different conception of character as well, for it forever altered our idea of the relationship between our inquiries and the world about and through which we make them. When we look at this series of events retrospectively, it is difficult not to see this shift as inevitable, even though it was not evident in the most obvious ways. Einstein was not inevitable any more than Boole was; nor was it inevitable that the key metaphor for the shift would be the theory of relativity. Nor, finally, was it inevitable that such a shift would take place when it did. It is conceivable that scientists like Einstein might have come up with a theory that would have allowed them to hold the Newtonian system together a while longer by patching it where there were holes. All of these "inevitabilities" were not inevitable; they were part of the human shape and character that the world took on through our inquiries into it, and there is nothing inevitable about the specific shape and character through which those inquiries are embodied.

What was inevitable about the shift was that sooner or later our ways of dealing with the universe would have had specifically to confront their own inadequacy and either decide to accept it or shift the nature of the questioning so as to overcome the perceived limitations. Einstein did not conduct his investigations with the idea that the Newtonian system was fatally flawed; he was working on local problems that he perceived as inadequate responses to the cruxes Newton's system revealed and did not see his work as an attempt to overturn Newton. But if he had not developed his special and general theories of relativity, sooner or later it would have become apparent that the problem resided within the Newtonian system itself rather than in the inability of scientists to question it properly. I am, of course, oversimplifying here inasmuch as Einstein was not working in a vacuum, and so he is here little more than a symbol for the shift that had to be recognized as inevitable and then either denied or affirmed. One could either choose to rewrite the novel of the world or resolutely stick to the old plot, but one way or the other the inevitability of that choice had to be faced because the free inquiry of science was always based on the earth that it sought to open up through its questions, because its free inquiry was always bound by that to which it addressed the question.

Science was and is based on the inevitability of accepting that which is, even if it assumed that by accepting the inevitable it could perhaps one day overcome it—if the "keys" to the universe were found, if the laws were properly located, then perhaps we could alter them to our own satisfaction and specification. The ironic result of the shift in science was that it immediately made those laws both more and less inevitable. The shift showed that we are not only essentially involved in our observations of the world, thus violating their purity, but also that we effect changes in the world through our participation in it. Some of the inevitability disappeared when it became clear that the way we live in the world affects the course of its events and thus alters its ontological structure— the world is not a mere description of the earth but rather changes the character of the earth through its descriptions and the application of them. For better or worse, this meant that man had a more serious stake in his descriptions than he thought he had, and this once again reveals the irony inherent in the objections of those who still wish to maintain the value of value-free inquiry: they would argue that to move in the direction I have outlined is to head into a world that is at once more determined and more dangerous. It is more determined to the extent that it requires accepting the inevitable and more dangerous because it seems to throw out all the rules of the game, leaving human choices in a horrible void where anything is possible. But the older, Newtonian conception of the world was more deterministic than the new one, and that was where its comfort lay, for we were seen merely to be describing invariant laws that always guaranteed the safety of our choices and that denied our effects in the world through our descriptions. In the guise of value-free inquiry, a severe determinism was offered that held the illusion of human con- straint clearly before the eye. The Einsteinian world is more dangerous precisely because we are now less determined while, on the other hand, we must still more strenuously accept the inevitabilities against which we have been fighting—our inability ever to catch up with the flow of the world, to escape its processes, and to construct a value-free system for dealing with them. What we really object to, then, is the shift in the nature of the inevitability that we must now confront and not the supposed lack of freedom inherent in it.

What this shift in the mode of science can most importantly reveal to us, however, is the consequence of accepting the difference of difference, for if it is true that much of the older science was devoted at least superficially to a struggle against inevitability, and if it is true that a great many things of value emerged from that mode of inquiry, then we must also come to see how it is not the only mode through which things of value emerge, and that things of greater value emerge from an inquiry that does not struggle against the inevitable but rather begins by accepting it. The key words of value here are *struggle* and *against,* for they suggest that our strength comes from the assertion of our powers against something just as they imply the need always to work against that which is. The metaphors of conflict and courage are so strong in these words that it is obvious where they derive their strength from. If the nature of existence is somehow inevitably embodied in conflict, however, as the difference of difference would imply because difference and conflict go hand in hand for us, how could we possibly be wrong in fighting against the difference, even if we recognize the struggle as a fight against the life instinct? Even if our struggle is based on our revulsion against time and the repetition compulsion of the death instinct, are not we more human because we fight in this manner? Inasmuch as the death instinct cannot be denied, should we not at least put it to use? These are difficult questions to avoid, particularly when they are, in effect, asserted vehemently by both those who espouse value-freeness and by those who espouse valuelessness. The nihilist would argue that inasmuch as there are no values, and inasmuch as every human action is an act of violence in any case, we may as well learn best how to make use of our violent choices. The humanist would argue that we need to preserve the values that generated all the great moments of our civilization, whatever the cost, because that which we have produced is so sublime that surely nothing better could be generated from a different value system. If pressed, the humanist would doubtless say that even if our actions have been based on the repetition compulsion of the death instinct and our struggle against life, that basis of action generated a Shakespeare, a Michelangelo, a Newton, and so how could we possibly choose another mode of proceeding when the fruits of the present one have been so magnificent? Only a fool would wish to deny the great human achievements of Western civilization, regardless of their origin or their goal. We know what our values have produced, and even if they have generated a great deal that is onerous as well, the strength of the real human achievements overrides any negative consequences that have also accrued as a result.

Faced with such arguments on either side, one must begin to wonder if the ultimate inevitability is the futility of the struggle against the value system that is based on the repetition compulsion. Even if it is true that the one side favors the repetition compulsion because it is satisfied with the fruits of it and unwilling to concede that something better might come from another system of values, and even if the other side favors the repetition compulsion because it seems naïve at this stage of human history to deny the fundamental relativism of human action and the violence that generates it, one must still wonder if these two opposite yet equal arguments are not compelling evidence in their own right that there is no middle ground, that the essential inevitability of human existence is that its fundamental mode of action is based on the repetition compulsion of the death instinct, on the revulsion against time, and on the struggle against life. While there is no guarantee that this is the case, these positions are at least identifiable and well known, and perhaps they are so because they are the only two conceivable ways of describing the nature of human activity. While there is thus much to suggest the inevitability of these positions, there is also no reason not to seek to discern whether there is another possibility, whether these values are not inevitable but simply part of a process of experimentation we have established as a result of the questions we have so regularly begun with. And inasmuch as at the very worst such inquiries would come to be seen as nothing more than one more link in the chain of the repetition compulsion, the questions seem well worth pursuing wherever they may go.

5 The Irony
of Openness

In order to chart the possibility of accepting the difference of difference without conceding the dominance of the death instinct, we should at first briefly delineate what has been invested in the power of the repetition compulsion, for even if it were conceivable for us to accept the inevitable, the history we have lived through has made this acceptance more difficult. Just over the past hundred years the changes in our thought have at once made acceptance of difference more possible by allowing its inevitability to emerge at the same time that the forces against its acceptance have hardened their positions. The arguments for denial are changed somewhat, but the roots of the denial remain the same. It may be more difficult today, for example, to argue for a theory of human progress than it was a hundred years ago, but this has only shifted the location of the argument, usually to some variant of the position I have already presented, that even if man has not progressed, his great achievements through the denial of difference have prevented him from falling back into the primeval slime, and the mode through which those accomplishments came to be ought thus be maintained if we are to prevent man from having an even worse fate than he now has. Equally implicit in this argument is the notion that to accept the difference of difference is to deny the great achievements of civilization, even though this does not necessarily follow, and even though it is equally possible to argue that only through these achievements have we been able to see the basis of our action in the world, a position that certainly does not devalue the work but rather puts it into a more compelling context by making it the framework that shows us how to respond to the world in a new way.

There can be no doubt, though, that an entire image of man

and human production is at stake here, just as the relations of power within human production are at stake. A great deal of that power resides in the idea of opposition, something we have come to see as courageous and strong, with no little reason inasmuch as there was—and continues to be—very much worth opposing in our social systems. If it could be said that opposition begins as an opposition to the brute facts of existence, a resistance against the forces of the earth against which we choose to struggle, yet it increasingly becomes transformed into the opposition of social systems that equally try to force certain brute facts of existence upon us against which we rightfully rebel. But in transferring this opposition to the social network, we have strengthened its power and so broadened its scope that we have come to see our relation to everything in the world as one of opposition, thus leading to the notion that it is the only stance one can properly adopt. The result is that we no longer have a clear idea of what needs to be opposed and what does not—we simply oppose everything in the belief that our only mode of power in the world comes through resistance. It becomes bad faith not to rebel against something, so opposition increases its power by regularly being defended in this way. Just as there are many who would say that giving up the notion of progress would consign man to inevitable decay, so there are those who would say that refusing to base one's actions on opposition is to do the same, for it would eventually lead to a capitulation to the worst instincts of man and to the acceptance of the status quo. To refuse to base every action on opposition is to be a reactionary force in the world in this context, for if one does not oppose everything one must make choices, and once one begins to consider one's choices outside of opposition, one will eventually come to rationalize proper opposition in terms of convenience. So one can either be a reactionary or a progressive force in the world, but one cannot deny the universality of opposition without becoming reactionary. Within this framework, the possibility is left out that one's opposition to things can emerge from one's acceptance of the inevitability of the difference of difference. Equally ignored is the fact that all opposition allows that which is opposed to define the terms of resistance and hence forces one to tie one's values to that which one opposes. Nevertheless, opposition itself, far more than any particular ideology or commitment, has such a polarized series of values built around it that it seems an almost insuperable obstacle. But the emotive force of the word and the underlying problems that are presented when one must seriously open up the process of making choices militate against opposing opposition.

The force of opposition is also strong because it is now inherently connected to our image of man. It may well be that those who established reason as the cornerstone of human existence did not intend to place man in opposition to the world, just as the scientist did not conceive of the objectivity that was conferred upon him in terms of opposition; but both reason and science did provide a model of man that made it possible for opposition to be seen as his most powerful characteristic. In isolating him from the world, and in arguing that he had the power to transcend his world, they focused on man as an isolable datum, as something that was independent of the scene over which he cast his glance. The result was that he inevitably spent his time observing himself. Even if there were not also godlike powers attributed to the view of man that emerged, his isolated position would inevitably lead man to see himself as a force over against nature and/or the social network that constantly eroded the value of reason. In centering man so, reason and science ended up making his oppositional character his chief attribute, even if this was not intended to turn him into a universal opposer.

Inasmuch as the centering of man was irretrievably connected to the view of man as opposer, it is now very difficult to imagine the one without the other, even though we now can see that man is the center of nothing, that indeed there is no center at all. It is one thing to see this, yet another to see the consequences of this for the view of man the opposer, and still another thing to be able to put into action a system of values not based on universal opposition. Because we unwillingly forego our position at the center of the universe, we make peripheral investments in opposition; because we fail to see that opposition is not a universal stance in man, we do not notice that all opposition is first of all based on the acceptance of something; and because we do not see that, we fail equally to begin to question that which needs to be accepted. It is a vicious circle with a logic of its own that is even more vicious because the basic connections are subterranean and all the more difficult to resist as a result. And the final irony of this position is that, being based on opposition, it accepts its differential relation to the world from the beginning, but it does so only to posit the vision of unity that will overcome the differential. It accepts its difference only to make possible the ultimate rejection of difference.

Opposition thus becomes connected to our notions of progress, even if we began by thinking that progress was a simple step-by-step process, a long line of continuities stretching to utopia. Instead, we begin to discern how progress is based on oppositions, on the overcoming of difference. Indeed, we come to see how it relies on overcoming the difference that we created at the outset in order to make progress possible: we establish our difference from the world in order ultimately to overcome both the difference and the world; we establish the difference in order to recuperate unity through progress. Progress was always a naïve notion to begin with, based as it was on the idea that everything else in the world remained static while we persistently built our way out of the world by understanding the forces that we had overcome. It was equally naïve to assume that all the vectors of change moved in one direction with the same force: if we are doing well at transforming the powers of the earth for our own purposes, then surely man as well is being transformed into a better state, that is, one in which he is more manipulable for our own purposes. Man thus became a plastic commodity just as the earth did; we conceived of ourselves as infinitely capable of change because we thought that our manipulations of the earth suggested that it was infinitely capable of change. Things could indeed be transformed, and we were learning the magic of transformation. Throughout all of this we failed to ask how much we were really transforming and how much was beyond our creative powers, and we forgot to ask this question of man as well, assuming that he could be made over as we saw fit. And inasmuch as we had invested so much in our belief in radical transformation, it was all the more a blow when we had to confront the fact that human nature did not seem to have changed very much over the centuries. Rather than investigating why this was the case, we simply inverted our sense of progress and argued that while man did not seem to have progressed very much over the past few hundred years, he would have regressed at an astonishing rate if we had not fought the good fight for human progress. This seems to be the inverted value we are left with today: we accept the illusion of progress, knowing it to be an illusion, in the belief that if we do not hold to it, man will become that much worse. Our opposition is now defined in terms of a resistance against negative progress, and the opposition increasingly appears to be the last line of defense against the hopeless nature of man.

We must ask ourselves, however, whether negative progress makes any more sense than its predecessor, and even more, we need to ask whether our great inventions have done anything at all to prevent man from slipping into negative progress. There can be no doubt that in one sense our technological transformations have made life "easier," for there is much we no longer need to concern ourselves with as a result of it. Food in Western countries is plentiful for most people, shelter is at least generally adequate, and so forth. Plagues have been minimized, some diseases eradicated, and this is all to the good, even if other diseases still grow, in part as the result of our transformations of the earth, in part simply because diseases still grow—they are most adaptable. Without even pursuing the negative effects that accrued as a result of these positive gains, though, we could see that these changes have done little to rectify that which we oppose in human nature. And if we were to inquire into the value of the great human productions of our epoch—the artistic accomplishments, the social and philosophical achievements—we would still be hard pressed to see them as a bulwark against negative progress. The world in which we live would certainly be less pleasing without them, but they have done nothing to make man more humane, so why should we think they have done very much to make man less humane? There is a sense in which they have kept the spirit of human greatness alive at a time when it is increasingly difficult to believe in it, and that is a positive value as long as we do not conceive of human greatness as godliness and as long as we do not fail to connect it to the other aspects of man. But one can assert the value of these human achievements without tying them to a concept of negative progress just as one can assert their value without tying it to a belief in human perfectibility. Human achievements do not have to be construed as necessarily based on the opposition of man to the inevitabilities of his existence any more than they need to be conceived of as monuments to man's futile fight against the "It was." We have chosen to see our accomplishments as based on opposition even if more times than not they are celebrations of what is rather than opposition to the way things are; we have preferred to believe that such celebrations are always wrested away from the forces of negativity in the world and have thus come to see them as man's essential assertion of immortality, as the consummate expression of his revulsion against time and its "It was." But even if an artist sees his work as a product of his revulsion against time, we do not have to agree with his sense of his work or be faced with denying the value of it. We can disagree with him and argue that, on the contrary, the beauty of his work is not based on a revulsion against time but rather on an acceptance and a celebration of it. Again, we choose not to see things this way because we have come to believe that our only strength resides in opposition, that our only human achievement is the ability to deny time in the face of our knowledge that we can never do so. And as long as human achievement is seen in terms of man's ability to deny the inevitable, we shall continue to perceive what man does in terms of negative progress and universal opposition to that which is.

Seen in this light, the surprising thing is not that many people have chosen to argue against values and assert the power of valuelessness; rather, it is astonishing that the upholders of value in our world can only do so by the most negative and nihilistic means possible. Construing the battle for value in terms of the seemingly ever-increasing trend toward valuelessness, they nevertheless fail to see their own position as essentially a negative one that concedes valuelessness but stresses the need to fight against the trend in spite of this recognition. So we are told that man's best fight occurs in opposition to the valuelessness that always surrounds him when in fact what is meant is that man's values are built out of opposition to his own intrinsic valuelessness. This is such a weak position that we should begin to wonder why it has any power over us at all, but then we realize that it does precisely because we believe that humans are essentially valueless, and believing that, we must hold on to this last line of defense in order to prevent what we always expect to happen anyway: the unleashing of the full force of human valuelessness without constraint. That conjures real fear in us, so we will readily enough cling to our opposition in spite of its absurdity.

The celebration of life as the struggle against, and therefore the momentary rising above, man's tendency to slip into valuelessness, an opposition to the inevitable that we hope we can keep deferring through regular glances at our icons of hope—this is the myth that oils the machine of values in our time, and it is as destructive a myth as one can imagine. But is it true that humans can only imagine and produce significant achievements by denying the death instinct that is at the heart of this view? Is it true that man cannot conceive of achievement without imagining a utopian world that denies life? And is it true that achievement is only possible by denying the inevitable rather than working out of it? Is all writing a writing against and for death? Is all painting? All other human accomplishment? Is there no other alternative?

We might at least try to imagine another possibility, beginning with an attempt to discern what is and is not inevitable so that we can decide whether or not we can accept it, and if we can, what the consequences for human achievement would be. The most inevitable thing in our life is time and its "It was." There is nothing we can do about time and its consequences. We can deny it, but only temporarily; we can ignore it, but only temporarily. We cannot forever be oblivious to its passing. Nor can we ultimately avoid the fact that our measure of time is also always passing. About this there seems to be little doubt, short of believing that we can freeze our bodies until humans eventually find a way to prevent cellular reproduction from breaking down. Within the world, time inevitably passes. This also means that there is always an "It was" about which nothing can be done. History can be rewritten, but the "It was" itself cannot be avoided. Nor can the effect of the "It was" on the present and the future be avoided; we can change the distribution of its effects according to our attitude toward it and according to the way we seek to plot a future in terms of it, and this makes the range of choice great indeed. But however wide the range of choice, and however it manifests itself, the "It was" will always exist in the present and the future. We get no clean slate as individuals or societies, and the "It was" is transmitted through everything we do, from our genes to our memories to our history books. It always writes itself into our future.

If time and its "It was" are inevitable, it also follows that human finitude is inevitable—the limit of personal time is death in the end and the contingencies of location while one is alive. There is, to be sure, no ironclad argument for the necessity of finitude beyond the obvious one: inasmuch as the history of man has always been determined by his finitude, if we were ever to find a means of transcending it, we would no longer be human. We would be something else altogether, for it is impossible to imagine the choices and values within the human domain as having any applicability in a world where man has transcended time. They would bear a metaphorical relationship to that new creature that, say, a lower primate's language "system" might bear to ours. In the most general of definitions, it could be said that a lower primate has a language, but not in a way that very much resembles human discourse. The same would be true for human values if man transcended time. Equally, it is true that man's *awareness* of his finitude is inevitable, for even though we can no doubt easily imagine a world where obliviousness has taken us over, it would again be the case that we would have ceased to be human.

Included within the inevitability of finitude is the inevitability of bodily limitation—there are some things that bodies are capable of doing and others they are not, and while the limits are once again flexible, depending on individual, historical, and social contexts, there are nevertheless definite limits. We are, for example, essentially rooted to the earth, and while it is possible to invent machines to allow us to fly, our bodies themselves are incapable of doing so, just as our various senses are incapable of being expanded beyond certain limits, though they can be enhanced through machines. Our bodies are also clearly bound to the inevitability of time and the "It was"—they have pasts to which they are attached, and futures that are in part limited by their "It was" and the inevitability of time.

Very few people would deny these inevitabilities. Admittedly, there are those who talk to god or have out-of-body experiences or believe that they have contact with other worlds, but these humans are in the minority, and even if they actually had such experiences, they would still be forced into the inevitabilities of time, the "It was," and the body. One can only understand, talk about, or otherwise make use of such experience through time. Beyond a general acceptance of these inevitabilities, however, lie the difficulties around which we have been circling, and the sense of inevitability becomes more problematic here. One could, like Freud, argue that there is a life instinct embodied in the pleasure principle that is inevitable, and however one chooses to describe such an instinct, one could certainly infer its plausibility on the basis of our awareness of nature, of reproduction, of the human species' inclination to reproduce itself regularly through time for quite a number of generations. Accepting this inevitability, however, unlike the other ones, would not mean that man could not overcome it—we have enough evidence around us in the form of nuclear weapons alone to convince us that it is indeed possible for man to overcome any life instinct in him, and particular kinds of suicide suggest the same possibility. If there is an inevitability to the life instinct, it can be overcome.

Like Freud, we could then proceed to declare the inevitabil-

ity of a death instinct too, and again there is compelling
evidence for its presence. We certainly can see it embodied
in any number of human endeavors, from the most basic
description of the repetition compulsion to the various ways
man has put such compulsions to work for him, granting that
quite often he does not necessarily see his behavior as a
manifestation of a death instinct. At the very least, though,
most of us would admit to having desires for closure, for the
end of life, whether we see them in terms of the closure we
put to use every day in the tasks we accomplish or in the
larger utopian dreams of a world devoid of fear, anxiety,
boredom, and the like. It seems plausible, then, that there is
something akin to what Freud termed the death instinct that
is inevitably inherent in man. It would also seem, like the life
instinct, that the death instinct can be overcome, even if death
itself cannot—no one can will himself not to die ultimately,
but one can recognize compulsive aspects of one's behavior
that are part of the death instinct and at least partially overcome them.

Finally, the inevitable would seem to extend to the inextrica-
ble relationship between the life and death instincts; the one
defines the other, so the one is not possible without the other.
Equally, the life instinct could not survive without the death
instinct because the death instinct is ultimately tied to the
inevitability of death, which is what allows new life to emerge.
What is less easy to discern is any kind of inevitable ratio
between the life instinct and the death instinct—we may well
hypothesize that inasmuch as there is still life, the life instinct
must always triumph over the death instinct, but inasmuch
as we are bound by our finitude, we have no way of knowing
this. We can develop plans of action based on one or the
other's predominating and test their value, but there is no
way ever finally to determine the ratio.

Another way of phrasing the inevitability of these inevitabilities is perhaps more fruitful and fundamental: the one
inevitability is the difference of difference. That distinction
allows time to emerge as the difference from timelessness; it
allows finitude to emerge as the difference of transcendence;
it allows the life instinct to emerge as the difference of the

death instinct; it allows man to emerge as the difference of the world; and finally, it allows man as self-awareness to emerge as the difference of man as body. It is not the case, however, that these differences themselves are inevitable, nor even ultimately fruitful. Likewise, the differences are not all of the same type. The man/world differential may be a valid one, for example, but only to the extent that the difference is bound to similarity as well: both are composed partly of organic material, for example. Their differential relationship is only adequate so long as it implies their essential similarities as well. The finitude/transcendence differential has a different quality to it, for "transcendence" is essentially a negative concept—it is defined as "not-finitude," "not-contingent," "not-limited," and so forth, and thus reflects finitude only through negativity. There is nothing finitude and transcendence have in common but their difference, while the man/world differential is defined in terms of both difference and similarity.

Regardless of the specific cases, the difference of difference is the inevitability out of which the relationship between terms emerges—after they have emerged in their differential relation, we can question what is and is not covered through the difference, but we need the difference in order to do that. One could go even further, as the poststructuralists have done, and argue that there is nothing more than the difference of language, but that is ultimately too claustrophobic a view. It would intrinsically make all differences equally valid or invalid, equally value-full or valueless outside of the arbitrary imposition of value onto certain differences that does not in fact reside in the difference itself. Such a view is ultimately akin to Sartre's early conception that man can make of himself what he chooses, though the poststructuralists, like the later Sartre, concede that the history of the self limits its freedom just as the history of value in certain differences informs their use in irretrievable ways. But if differences are bound only by their history and man's arbitrary use of them, our transformations of the world would all be equally effective or ineffective, and that is not the case. Some differences—the man/world difference, for example—were able to be invested with great value, however fundamentally flawed they were. Man in this case used the difference to generate a considerable series of changes in his world, whereas other differences—the finitude/transcendence one, for example—while invested with great value, ultimately came to nothing when half of the differential could never be filled out. The poststructuralists too easily assume that all differences are based on the finitude/transcendence model, where one term is essentially a void; they fail to recognize that some differences, like the man/world relation, are based on fulness as well as lack, on similarity *and* difference.

If we wish to say that the difference of difference is inevitable, then, we would still need to locate those differences that are inevitable, and they would be bound up in time and the "It was," human finitude, and the life and death instincts. Time itself is an essential aspect of the difference of difference because difference always involves deferral, the intrusion of time—the "It was" is the essential basis of deferral, as that which is always deferred through the passing of time into the future. Human finitude is essential to difference because man can conceive of things only in terms of difference because he is finite; in other words, he is finite because he is that creature who allows the difference of difference to emerge. The life and death instincts are intrinsic to the difference of difference because time can only pass as long as there is life and can only be denied through death. Whereas the difference of difference can in one sense be conceived of as the only ultimate inevitability, it can only be sensible to the extent that its inevitability is connected to the inevitability of the others. The difference of difference, that is, makes no sense unless it is defined in terms of time, the "It was," human finitude, the body, and some concept like the life and death instincts.

Given these basic inevitabilities, and some that follow from them—for example, that man is intrinsically bound to language—we have generally defined the range of the inevitable. Beyond these constraints and their corollaries, man has considerable freedom of choice. Nevertheless, these inevitabilities bind man more than he would like, and in some views the goal of life seems to be little more than fighting against these constraints. What we now need to ask is whether or not human existence ought necessarily be defined in terms of fighting against these inevitabilities; whether or not the best that is thought and said necessarily derives from a struggle against these constraints; in short, whether the human conception of the good, the true, and the beautiful must always necessarily be seen in terms of the death instinct and the revulsion against time, or whether it is possible to conceive of a definition of the good, the true, and the beautiful that begins by accepting the life instinct and time even as it accepts the inevitability of the death instinct.

If one begins with the difference of difference, accepting it and the life instinct of which it is a part, one also accepts that one's productions in the world are a product of that acceptance. Only by agreeing to live in time can one profit fully from the "It was" that is a part of it; only by agreeing to live in time can one put the full measure of one's finitude to use. In denying time, one is only forced to accept it in the end anyway, and in denying finitude one is only forced more resolutely back to it, though the denial makes one's finitude seem a prison of incapability rather than a limit that marks the region of productive activity. In denying time and finitude, one learns for the most part only that time and finitude cannot be denied, and one also comes to despair over the limits that can never be transcended. In accepting time and finitude, one still has to investigate their limits, for they are constantly changing, but one can see the development to and out of the limits in terms of antecedents—in building to the limit rather than trying to overreach it, one can establish a sense of how one gets there and of what one can do when one arrives. The basis of the recursive question, upon which the difference of difference and the acceptance of time and finitude are based, is that all questions move to the limit; they return only when the limit has been reached, only when they must circle back to trace the pattern with a difference. Far from being a mode in which one decides at the outset what the limits are and then refuses to probe them, the recursive question inevitably moves to the limit, moves from a particular context to the limit of the orientation that is present within it. In this, its chief difference from the discursive question is that it is more interested in what opens up on the way to the limit than it is in what lies beyond it inasmuch as it concedes from the outset that what lies beyond is by definition outside its purview.

In being more concerned with what opens up on the pathway of a particular context as it builds to the limit, the recursive question focuses on that which the discursive denies, the value of the way there. Instead of working out of a context in the hope of transcending it, the recursive seeks to see what can be done from within that context. It thus affirms its process rather than the end and accepts that its value derives from what develops through the activity of questioning rather than the residue left over when the question has reached the limit and returns. And again unlike the discursive, the recursive has built into it the knowledge that the return from the limit will have changed the context from which it began—it will always return with a difference, for the difference is that which has developed through the process of questioning and is thus the yield of understanding that changes the context and makes the next question begin from a different location. The discursive sees its questions as value-free—they do, after all, seek to transcend context, and their goal is to keep value out of view, to end up with a residue of "knowledge" that is not intrinsically connected to the values of a question. This is why the discursive must always deny the value of the process of questioning itself—it must look at the questions as always the same, as repetitions of each other, for otherwise the residue will be bound to the context and will not be repeatable. To accept the value of the process of questioning itself—and the values embodied in particular questions—is to concede from the beginning that the residue will always be different, hence not repeatable, hence caught in time. Purity depends upon ignoring the process and focusing on the end alone.

In accepting time and finitude, in beginning from and working through and returning within them, one finds one's interest in what develops along the way and seeks new ways to put what develops along the way to use, but this can only be done because one has accepted that what is gained along the way introduces differences that forever change the context from which one began. In one way, this is to concede no more than the obvious: questions are instruments that affect that which is questioned. They do not pass through the terrain they set out on without leaving a mark; they alter it in passing through it. This makes sense inasmuch as the question is not asked with knowledge of its answer already available—one asks it because one seeks to understand what will be uncovered in the process of questioning. And inasmuch as the process has an orientation, it will establish the path of the question in terms of the difference inherent in the orientation and thus lead one where one has never been before—the "answer" is more the differential pathway that is opened up than anything else, though the difference is marked by the limit of the question.

Returning from one more angle, we can see that the acceptance of time and finitude means that the question begins not from a perspective of opposition but from difference. Man as questioner establishes his difference by asking the question—stones do not ask questions, nor do molecules—but the difference of the question presupposes an essential relationship between questioner and that which is questioned. The recursive does not place man over against the world and does not conceive of the process of questioning as a dialectical battle between master and slave wherein man tries to assert his mastery over the world while the world tries to assert its mastery over man, the temporary victor in this dialectic being decided by the nature of the answer at the end of the question. The recursive is dialectical, but it proceeds under the assumption that the question is the differential that allows both man and world to emerge in a new way precisely because of their differences. The recursive question is not oriented toward declaring a victor—as we see in that the answer is less important than the pathway opened up—but rather in seeing what productive capabilities are allowed to emerge through the orientation of the question. Man and world are defined through the differential that the question establishes rather than the other way around, and thus the question provides a productive interchange between man and world that allows aspects of each to be uncovered. The differential of recursivity means that man and world are oppositional without being opposed; their strength and productivity come from working within the differential rather than in opposition to it.

Psychologically, the acceptance of time and finitude places man in the world rather than in opposition to it. In so doing, it puts an end to our naïve ideas of autonomy, but it also delivers us from the bondage of alienation. Autonomy/alienation is that differential through which man sought to dominate the world and to deny the dialectic of difference, but as the orientation that autonomy/alienation provided became less and less effective, the sense of autonomy diminished as the master/slave dialectic could less and less be denied, while the alienation remained and grew. Alienation, as the last defense of autonomy, denies autonomy by crying out against isolation, seeking interconnectedness by attempting to conquer the master/slave dialectic in one grand assertion of power. But the acceptance of time is the denial of autonomy and alienation; one can neither be autonomous nor alienated, even if one may construe one's relations to the world in this way. On the other hand, the differential of finitude means that the seeming goal of the alienated—complete union—is also impossible, for one is always related through one's difference rather than overcoming it—it is the difference itself that makes relation possible, and so it cannot be negated without denying relation altogether, the pathway of alienation. One would thus be inclined to say that the acceptance of time and finitude is healthier as an orientation—and leads to more productive activity—inasmuch as it does not force one into the solipsism of alienation and the desire for revenge that alienation generates.

Inasmuch as the acceptance of time and finitude is based on focusing on the process of the question and what develops from it, though, we need to question its productive capacity more in order to determine the limits of its power. For if one focuses on the process of questioning rather than on the answers, one is concentrating on the present through which one lives—that is, after all, what accepting time and finitude means—and in stressing the present, one seemingly loses sight of the past and the future. This idea is reinforced via the discursive through the argument that the best that is thought and said has always been accomplished through a denial of the present and a postulation of some utopian future. Underlying this argument is the notion that one can only hope to make a better future by denying the present, that one can only move into the future in a mindless way if one lives in the present, taking what comes to one rather than giving shape to one's own life. But this argument is either absurd or else a rationalization of the revulsion against time—absurd because even in denying the present one is still living through it, rationalization of the revulsion against time because it seems to offer transcendence in the present through a denial of it and transcendence in the future as the utopian goal that is arrived at through the denial.

The recursive nonetheless is indeed a mode that focuses on the present, on the process through which one questions and thus establishes the differentials through which one lives. But the acceptance of time and finitude also means the acceptance of the "It was" and thus signifies that one's present must always be seen in the context of the "It was" out of which it emerges and through which its present and future plans are given shape. The limits of finitude are in one sense defined by the "It was" and the future that is always the limit into which one is moving, so the acceptance of time necessarily requires one to mark the present in terms of the past, and the direction of the future is determined by the relation between the "It was" and the present.

This is readily apparent when we turn to the recursivity that is part of the acceptance of time, for it has embedded within it the necessary relation of the present to the "It was" and the future. The recursive assumes the necessity of a context—all questions begin from a specific location, which is nothing more than the "It was" itself—the context is the "It was" as it presents itself from a particular location, and as such all questions that proceed on their pathways begin with the "It was" that led to them in the first place. Likewise, the "It was" leads into the future through the question that situates it. One does not mindlessly move into the future; instead, one moves into it on the basis of the question that was in the first place a formulation of one's understanding of the "It was" in terms of one's own situation. The question is a direction through the present into the future based on the differences that have emerged from the past out of which the question arose. The process of the question is thus a questioning of the future and the possibilities that might emerge from the differences the question generates. Equally, the future that emerges through the differences is also a questioning of the "It was," for the process of inquiry tests the values that are embodied in the differences themselves. Thus, if a particular mode of questioning and its orientation do not seem to "lead" anywhere—if we are dissatisfied with where we have come on the basis of them, we question the "It was" out of which they came in order to discern what might be problematic in them. The recursive question can lead to differences that are ineffective just as much as it can open up a valuable pathway; it too is finite and therefore can always take us to a location of little value. And indeed, to some extent this is true of every question. In the process of questioning, not everything works, and the return of the query always forces us to discern what did and did not seem effective, thus addressing the "It was" out of which the question came. If the question always returns with a difference, that difference can be defined as the relationship between what worked—what confirmed our sense of the "It was," and what is different, that is, what would have been unexpected in terms of the "It was" with which we began. The difference in the return always leads us to revise our understanding in order to account for the difference.

Far from leading us away from the past and the future, focusing on the question keeps us from forgetting them; it is the process through which we come to understand them as we revise our questions in terms of the difference in the return. The recursive thus makes questioning understandable as an activity, whereas the discursive can only refer to the "trial and error" or "hit and miss" technique, two orientations that are sometimes characterized as "methods," but which in

fact are descriptions of the discursive's failure to account for
its own method. The discursive cannot account for itself because it refuses to accept the process of method—in order to
deny its involvement in process, it must see its activity in
terms of discrete, binary events—something either works or
it does not, and if it does not, one tries something else; if
it does, one tries the same thing again. "Trial and error"
demonstrates the ignorance of method through its binary
chopping and equally denies the reasonable nature of its proceedings by tacitly accepting that trial and error must rely on
intuitive leaps by the questioner. The recursive makes sense
out of these leaps by describing the process through which
they occur, and it also makes better sense out of the relation
of the process of questioning to the "It was" and the future
because it does not deny its essential connection to them.

Put more generally, one could say that the recursive offers
a better view of human existence because it accepts the basis
of it rather than denying it. In accepting time, it is able to
make sense out of the relationship between past, present, and
future, it can describe the process in an intelligible way, and
it puts past and future to work in the present. Unlike the
discursive, which is based on the denial of the present, the
present is the focus of the recursive, but unlike the nihilistic
point of view, the focus on the present does not lead to a
rejection of past and future.

Having accepted time and finitude, we find our place in the
world equally altered. Because the earth is necessarily a part
of the "It was" that man must accept, he seeks to work in
consort with it rather than trying to dominate its forces purely
for his own purposes. Inasmuch as the question opens up the
world as much as it opens up man, and inasmuch as the one
opening cannot be separated from the other, man sees his
productive energies as a result of the opening up and an
extension of the understanding he arrives at through the
enframing of the question itself. And because the productive
energies are a part of the opening up of the question rather
than its resolution, man's productions become tied to what is
possible within the frame of the question rather than to the
imposition of a frame on the earth that is designed only to

extract productions from it. The discursive construes its questions sequentially, and it sees the answer to the question as the end, so it employs its queries momentarily to frame something within the earth in order to remove what is valuable from the frame. The frames are not seen as residing in time, and each one is independent of the others, so no thought is given to the relation of one to another or to the time of the earth. This makes sense insofar as the goal of the discursive is to make use of the earth, for it is not considered an essential aspect of a differential relation but rather as something inert to be exploited by the power of man. And because man fails to see the differential relation through the discursive, he also ignores how his practices affect the earth and himself just as he fails to see how the earth fights back against his attempts at dominance.

Within the recursive, the value of what is opened up in man and earth is always questioned, always returned to, and thus what emerges is more likely to be consonant with the valuable aspects of both. The differential effect is a sign of respect, for in recognizing the necessity of this tie, man is forced to see that his own fate rests on that which he allows to emerge through his questions. He must serve the earth as it serves him, so he considers what is best suited to the opening of the earth through the question. This does not mean, of course, that he "censors" his questions and falls back in fear of the earth's reciprocity, thereby refusing to push an inquiry to the limit. Rather, the orientation of the question—in its acceptance of the differential—allows the earth to emerge in a way that precludes arbitrary slicings into and arbitrary extractions from it. The "It was" always contains the history of our questions within it, and we base our present inquiries on this history, so we always have a general idea of the range of our questions even as we seek to extend it. We know where to begin within this differential in order to extend it where we have not been before.

This is not to say that the recursive is a foolproof mode of opening up the earth in ways that are necessarily always full of value. The limit of the context of the question and the difference of the return preclude any perfect means of dealing with the earth. The recursive, if you will, generates "mistakes" as much as the discursive does. It is simply that the recursive, in always returning to the question, is more conscientious in probing the mistakes that a question has generated. And its awareness of the limit of context always leads it to question other contexts for their difference. Because it is equally aware of the fact that its questions always have consequences, it seeks to understand them as much as possible. As a result, the consequences of man's mistakes are equally unavoidable; the positive value in mistakes is that they make future questions more precise, but the residue of the mistake cannot be simply discarded. It must be attended to by placing it back into the context out of which it came and questioning it once again.

From the discursive point of view, this attitude toward the earth is altogether too servile in its implications. One can well imagine a question arising of this sort: where would man be today if he had taken a respectful attitude toward the earth? None of his major transformations of it would have been possible, and he would be living in a most primitive world. Respect for the earth is for environmentalists and mystics and has nothing, thank god, to do with man's future. But it does not follow from the recursive that the earth shall not be opened up via the transformations of man; indeed, the very basis of the recursive is that the earth is always first opened up to the transformations of which it is capable through the questions of man. The recursive simply concedes the complexity of the earth's texture and of man's relation to it rather than assuming that man's simple manipulations upon it are truly simple. In conceding that human questions have consequences, though, the recursive does not turn away from opening up the earth—it merely seeks to do so in a way that takes into account as much as possible the effects man has through his questioning just as it seeks to reveal the value of the questions man raises. The older mode of inquiry gave no thought to the values of the question—if it could be done, there was no reason not to try it. The absence of responsibility inherent in that kind of questioning is what the recursive attempts to overcome.

The recursive, then, accepts that all questions are in one sense a violence committed on the earth—they are ruptures, openings within its tissue that would not exist without the question. In another sense, however, such ruptures are not generically different from the other eruptions of life on earth. To the extent that the question is a rupture, it is no more of one than the reproduction of life itself, which, through the difference of re-production, is always generating the new. It is true that man is capable of more intrusive ruptures precisely because of his questions, but from the recursive view the ruptures are grafts as well as separations; they seek to generate the new rather than destroy the old, and as such man's most productive power in the world comes from the grafts of his questions that are at once rupture and the generation of the new through the conjoining of difference. To focus only on the rupture and not the graft, to fail to see that rupture can also be graft, and to ignore the fact that the grafting of difference is a process of life to be distinguished from the rupture of violence, separation and isolation is to concede the nihilistic argument that the life instinct and the death instinct are indistinguishable and that one is of equal value to the other. Likewise, to see the graft only as graft without rupture is to ignore the value-full nature of all grafting, as the discursive practitioners would like to do—in ignoring the rupture, they can also ignore value and consequence. Theirs is a value-free act that escapes the violence of rupture, or so they would like to think.

Finally, it would be absurd to argue that science as we know it would be impossible within the framework of the recursive simply because at its most profound levels it has always been recursive to begin with. This is not to say that scientists have necessarily been aware of the recursivity inherent in their practice—many have not. Many have chosen to see the brilliance of science in its isolation and exploitation of difference and have failed to notice that the theory of science is always based on the difference of difference, on the inevitable differential that can never be isolated into separate constituents. The stated goals of science—which are to break everything into its discrete parts while also accounting for the unity underlying all difference—have certainly been at odds with scientific theory and practice, but the practice itself has been recursive regardless of the stated goals. Scientists have not questioned the values of their questions, nor have they investigated the values underlying their goals, believing their enterprise to be value-free, but they have not been able to escape their values even when they have tried, as their own questioning about the responsibility they hold for the consequences of their speculations shows. Believing that their practice is totally discursive, they have thus not found a way to deal with the values in their recursive practice, but their questions have been recursive for all that. It is simply time to recognize and accept the values inherent in the practice, not so we can deny science but rather so we can begin more seriously to consider what it does and should do, what questions are appropriate, and how one's orientation to those questions ought to be considered. All sciences, after all, are as much a part of the social network as they are investigations of the earth; they are implicated in the development of man as much as they are involved in the development of the earth, and this need not constrict the scientist's activity—it ought, on the contrary, to give it a greater sense of direction inasmuch as the full stakes of the game are known when it accepts its complicity in values. What these values mean in terms of the particular productive capabilities of science remains to be seen, but inasmuch as its own findings have turned it toward the recursive, certainly it needs to reconsider the nature of its practice.

It is certainly true that science is a part of the social network and needs to be considered in that light, but we also need to reflect on the relation of the recursive to the social network, for it is one thing to speculate about the changes in man's orientation toward himself and the earth that occur with the acceptance of time and finitude, and it is another, more complex problem to see how the acceptance of difference affects man's relation to other humans. The most obvious point to make would be that the acceptance of time and finitude by no means necessitates acquiescence in the face of the social network. In accepting the differential relationship, one also

concedes that the differences are not hierarchically maintained, that they are not brought under the sway of the mas-
ter/slave dialectic but rather allowed to emerge outside of a
dominance/submission position. Inasmuch as all too much of
the social network is based on just such an abuse of difference,
the acceptance of time and finitude ought to lead to opposition
to that which refuses to accept time and to that which denies
temporality through the master/slave dialectic in whatever
form it manifests itself. This, however, is not an opposition
for opposition's sake, nor is it a mode of resistance that seeks
to appropriate the position of that which it opposes. To do so
would only be to accept the role of slave and the desire to be
master, which would equally be a denial of time. One must
oppose the dialectic without assuming a position within it,
yet this raises problems of its own, for there is then the
question of how an effective opposition can develop that does
not take up its part in the master/slave dialectic. Our own
history suggests that the way to oppose the master is first of
all to accept the role of his slave and then fight against his
mastery, seeking to overturn it. We know that this is eventually an effective means of ridding ourselves of the master—
at least temporarily. Unfortunately, we also know that it is
difficult to put off the role of the master once it has been
appropriated, and inasmuch as that is equally a denial of time,
nothing much has been achieved through the reversal except
that for a while one is able to think that the problem has been
resolved.

On the other hand, an opposition that denies the opposition
is not effective either. First of all, it is a naïve position, for one
can never negate the opposition any more than one can deny
one's connection to the social network. The "It was" necessarily involves one in both, regardless of one's desires. To create
the illusion that this is not the case is thus equally to deny
time, for one must renounce one's connection to the "It was"
in order to maintain the illusion. Additionally, even if the
illusion did not involve one in the denial of time, the effectiveness of the position would be minimal at best. It would avoid
that which should be faced rather than accept the necessary
opposition to it, and the result would be purely negative. This

too seems an inadequate way to respond to that which needs to be opposed through the acceptance of time and finitude.

The option that remains seems, for better or worse, simply to assert the difference of one's difference, simply to live the life of acceptance of time and finitude without disguising it as an attitude of either the slave or the master. Inasmuch as such a life is oriented toward the possibilities that are opened up through the difference of difference, and inasmuch as it is directed to discerning the value of what is opened up, it necessarily places one in a participatory role in the world, and that has effects in its own right, unlike the simple passivity of the opposition that denies the opposition. Likewise, the orientation to the life that is allowed to emerge through the opening of one's questions precludes one's stance from being an isolated series of actions. To assert the difference of difference is to place oneself in a certain relation to the abuse of difference, and this means that one's assertion of the difference of difference must be taken up by those who deny time and abuse difference. To place oneself before the abuse of difference without abusing it is necessarily to question the way the world is enframed through its abuse—it calls attention to the limits and abuses of difference without putting one in the position of the slave. It may well be that those who see themselves as masters interpret one's position as that of the slave, but the insistent assertion of the difference of difference is the only way to convince them otherwise.

It is necessary to stress, though, that the assertion of the difference of difference is an attitude or an orientation, not a series of affectations one might adopt in order to emphasize one's uniqueness. The purpose of the attitude is not to dramatize one's own difference—that is to become part of the master/slave dialectic. One does not seek to stand out, a strategy of opposition that is easily dealt with, particularly in the era of life-styles, in which one's opposition is merely seen as an alternate life-style and therefore quickly dismissed. In asserting the difference of difference, one may well stand out, however, and this complicates one's position, for it is the difference of difference that needs to be highlighted rather than the one who opens up the context. Trained as we are in the symbology of individual difference, we tend automatically to interpret it as a reflection of character alone when in fact it ought to be construed in terms of the nature of the difference itself.

The goal of accepting difference within the social network is thus devoted to a full range of participation within it—one must involve oneself in the differences that are available in order to assert the difference of difference. And inasmuch as the difference of difference means that one always only *is* in terms of one's differential relationship with the world, there is no such thing as a private stance or attitude—all orientations can only be effective to the extent that they demonstrate the impossibility of having a private position on and in the world.

There are, of course, some large and compelling problems in the assertion of the difference of difference, beginning with the almost inevitable tendency for it to be interpreted as yet one more stance within the master/slave dialectic and continuing on up to the question of what kind of change can be introduced into the social system through such an attitude. In what might almost be the best of cases, the assertion of difference is seen for what it is, but then it is perceived as merely mysterious because it does not make sense within a discursive view of the world. The difference is carried across, but understanding does not go beyond the awareness of it as a difference that cannot be appropriated into the conventional symbolic network. Some value is brought to light, but the crucial worth of the position remains hidden in mystery. This mystery can only be overcome through the continual assertion of difference, though that is no guarantee of effectiveness— the difference of difference could still remain a cipher. There is again the possibility of simple misinterpretation, the tendency to reduce the assertion to a difference of life-style, thus rendering it as harmless as a safety pin through the cheek. There is also the possibility that the assertion of difference will be seen for what it is and be perceived as a threat: while the assertion of the difference of difference is an acceptance of time and thus a denial of the spirit of revenge—and the envy and resentment that are bound up with it—its very acceptance of time can generate the envy and resentment that it has denied, thus leading it to be seen as something that must be overcome so as to revenge the other's awareness of his denial of time. The assertion of difference, in other words, can be construed as an arrogation of power that undermines another's sense of his masterful role; his assurance of mastery is called into question by the assertion of difference, for he is forced to confront his denial of time, so the assertion needs to be put out of play in some way so he can avoid his own negation. There is, in short, no guarantee of the effectiveness of the assertion of difference; or rather, there is a guarantee of effectiveness but none that it is the effectiveness one desires.

The same thing can be said for the larger question of how a social network can be conceived on the basis of the difference of difference rather than the denial of it. The greater complexity of the social system makes the tracing of effectiveness much more difficult and the institution of questions of difference much more problematic. There can be no specific programs of action that would lay out in advance an itinerary for addressing these problems because any such program would negate the difference of difference by denying the "It was" through the imposition of a structure in the face of our thorough inability as finite creatures ever to impose such constructs.

The crucial question here, however, is whether any course of action can be developed from the difference of difference. The first thing that needs to be reiterated is that the acceptance of the difference of difference means that one must accept the death instinct. Inasmuch as it is part of the differential that includes the life instinct, it cannot be denied. One's own finitude forces one to confront the limit of context and death, and man has an unavoidable tendency to want to leap over these encumbrances. Likewise, given the difference of difference, one can only accept time by recognizing one's tendency to deny it; otherwise the acceptance of time would mean nothing. If it could be accepted once and for all, irrevocably, its acceptance would be a denial of difference, for it is only because one must repeatedly accept it through the difference of denial that it has any significant value. This means that the tendency toward the revulsion against time never disappears; the acceptance of temporality must continually be asserted over against the powerful desire to deny time. Likewise, unlike the ultimate Marxian state, this means that the desire for revenge never withers away; it is always that over against which one must assert one's acceptance of life.

In the acceptance of time, there are no final victories because one can only accept it by acceding to the difference of difference that involves one in the death instinct and the life instinct alike. If there is an advantage to the acceptance of time, then, it is not that it eliminates the difference, which was always the goal of the discursive network; it is rather that in accepting the difference of difference one allows life to assert itself over death so that the difference of difference can emerge as an oppositional relationship that is dialectical without being a part of the master/slave network. The paradox here is that this differential relationship can only be possible if life first asserts its mastery over death, for only through that assertion can one overcome the otherwise inevitable and infinite unfoldings of the spirit of revenge. It could doubtless be said that this paradox requires one always to valorize one aspect of a differential relation over another and is thus in effect really only another denial of the difference of difference, and if one does not accept the paradox this is doubtless true.

The only defense against such an argument is that the alternative involves one in a paradox as well. One could simply throw oneself into the play of difference without regard for what way the differences will be played out, but in so doing one must commit oneself to the force of the master/slave dialectic without regard for its consequences. To throw oneself into the play of difference does not eliminate the master/slave dialectic; rather, it makes one a slave to it and simply valorizes the virtues of the slave. The other possibility is regularly to devote oneself to the explication of differences that valorize the master's position while decrying the mastery of his position, arguing that it should not be so valorized— but this is ultimately only to echo the cry of the slave who desires to be master, who wishes that the exclusions inherent in the master's valorization of the differential worked the other way. Decrying the exclusionary practices of the master without denying the necessity of them once one is within the master/slave dialectic is simple hypocrisy once one understands the nature of these exclusionary networks. And if each of these positions forces one in one way or another to confront the paradox of one's view; if, in short, it is impossible to avoid a paradox if one pushes the difference of difference to its limit; then one must choose which paradox to accept. The choice of paradox is thus inevitable, short of a willful ignorance, and if this is indeed so, then it seems that the only choice to make is the one that accepts time and finitude without denying the essential presence of the death instinct as well. The only other alternatives are to pretend that a choice is not necessary or to act as though humans must give up their self-consciousness and the responsibility it involves them in by throwing themselves up to the infinite play of difference without regard for the manner in which the differences are played out. Perhaps the final fraudulence in that view is that it accepts the death instinct by seeking to deny the self-consciousness that makes one aware of it, thus eradicating the need to deal with it.

In any case, the limits of the inevitable inherent in the difference of difference do not preclude the acceptance of time and the assertion of it over against the denial of time. In fact, the recursive—as the mode through which the difference presents itself—is also that mode that accepts time by measuring the cycle of return and the difference within it. It is always the difference within the return that allows time to be marked in the first place, and so to accept the difference of difference is to accept time as the measurement through which life asserts its priority over death. The limit of difference is that which pushes time to the limit and thus makes life's possibilities emerge to their limit as well because it is only through the limit of difference and its continual reassertion that the repetition compulsion of the death instinct is brought under the sway of the return with a difference, overcoming the repetition and the compulsiveness at its center.

There may well be no guarantee of the ultimate priority of the recursive difference, then, but it does bring a coherence to man's activity that is not found within the discursive, and it opens up possibilities that differ from the repetitions that ceaselessly pour forth from the discursive. Man may make of these possibilities what he will, but the acceptance of time and finitude at least seems to offer a view of man more consonant with that which we have already come to understand. If its limits and capabilities and the efficacy of its premises have yet to be adequately tested, this simply suggests the strength of man's resistance against that which he has always known was inevitable in any case. While the strength of the resistance might suggest that we ought not to probe too deeply into that which man has always tried to ignore, the increasing consequences of our refusal to confront it and the ever-insistent return of time with a force that cannot be denied might more seriously suggest that it is time to confront the recursive and learn to accept the inevitable limits of time and finitude that make the productivity of man possible in the first place. It may be true that up to this point it has never yet been too late to do this, but there is no guarantee that this will always be so.

6 Questioning as Quest

In "The Question Concerning Technology" and other essays, Heidegger attempts to discern what kind of world we have made for ourselves and suggests that the questions we have framed have led to an increasingly inert context: our questions no longer call forth the earth in a productive and meaningful way. Instead, we have brought to the fore things that now threaten the earth and our place within it. Our enframing of the world brought much to light, but it has also come to threaten life itself, and inasmuch as this is true, we must begin to ask ourselves how we can better go about constructing the world in which we live. At the heart of this problem lie the nature of the question and the quest that underlies all queries. If the discursive mode of questioning has taken us this far, it is also increasingly clear that it cannot carry us much farther by itself, for the dilemmas it has created surround us in so many ways that we no longer know how to deal with them. The machine that we devised to eliminate the contradictions in the world has led to so many contradictions that we seem hemmed in on every side—the light of our questions has always turned back to reveal the dark underside that we sought to escape.

If the stakes of our questions now seem more crucial than ever before, this is because we have saturated the earth with our inquiries to an unprecedented degree and have arrived at the point where every crux in the world seems related to every other one: there are no longer neatly separable problems to deal with in their own local space, for the local space has come to involve everything. To a certain extent, this is doubtless true for every human epoch, for most periods of history have left man feeling that the stakes of his questions are crucial, and this is not surprising simply because on an individual basis the same situation has always prevailed. There comes a time in many people's lives when they begin to see that the questions they have been trying to deal with separately are irretrievably connected just as there comes a time when one begins to see the implications of the questions one has been asking and the consequences they have on the way one lives one's life. It is not difficult to reach a point where an individual sees that his questions do have consequences for the way he lives; indeed, it is almost inevitable. We may all begin throwing questions out to the world in a seemingly random manner, but most of us arrive at the moment when we realize that our questions were not merely random and that they had everything to do with the shape of our lives. We come to realize that they are not value-free, and then we have to ask whether we like where they have taken us. The problem is that while most of us will reach this point, it is not inevitable that we will agree to see the consequences of what we are. We can always turn away. When our lives have become filled out enough to see where we have been and to show where we are likely to go, we can either ask questions about our direction or turn away from such queries.

The same process occurs on a historical level as well, and there are many periods of human history that have been sufficiently filled out to lead to serious questions about the direction and shape of the world in which we live. In our own time, in the middle of all the transformations generated by discursive practice, the life of the world is more filled out than ever before, so the consequences of our questions have become that much greater. The dilemmas we face are not new, but the results of the way we deal with them spread their force over a much wider domain. Humans, for example, have regularly worried about the destruction of their world, but no humans have been better equipped to destroy life than those who are living now. As a result, our questions have taken on greater significance than ever before, so we are left with the option of assuming the greater responsibility that goes along with this or seeking to ignore it.

Nietzsche's way of presenting the issue of our responsibility and our location in the world was through the distinction between the last man and the overman. For him, our questions had led to the point where there was a crucial threshold between the way we are and the way we must be if we are to survive the consequences of what we have been. To call for the overman is to state unequivocally that we can no longer go on as we have, that we have reached the point where man is no longer sufficient for the world he has made. Another way of putting this is simply to state that humanity has reached a certain state of maturity on this planet—maturity being measured by the inescapable consequences of one's actions in the world—and man is now faced with the decision to accept his maturity or reject it. The question then is the same one that we as individuals all face at certain points in our lives: can we bear to live with our maturity? Can we bear to live in a world where our actions have consequences and we must not only accept them but also consider which consequences we should like to generate? Put this way, the problem perhaps seems less important than it is, but I phrase it that way only because it really makes it as important as it can be. As Milan Kundera says in *The Book of Laughter and Forgetting*, we live in a time where man seems increasingly to be returning to infancy rather than accepting maturity, where the need to forget is stronger than ever, where forgetfulness is encouraged not only by ourselves as individuals but also by the state. And we drift toward infancy precisely so that we do not have to accept our maturity as individuals or as a species. We encourage forgetfulness so that we do not have to remember our responsibility; we forget in order to deny time and the "It was," for they are the mark of our acceptance of responsibility at the same time that they seem so filled out and overwhelming—the moment of maturity—that it is all the more difficult to forget them. Given this, Nietzsche may well have been right to stress the great difference between the last man and the overman, for the gap between the two increases the more we choose to forget, the more we return to infancy.

The quest for the overman means that we must accept the relationship between the quest and our questions and the consequences that come from their connectedness. Questions are questings by nature, and man as questioner quests by nature, but no quest ever turns out as we had planned and all of them reach the point of maturity where we must recognize where we have come and how we want to proceed from where we are. To accept our questing nature is simply to accept our thrownness—our questions are always leading out into a world that we do not fully comprehend, and our quests are always a projection of our thrownness, a moving out from a place we do not fully know into one we do not fully know either. The difficulty is that we tend to see our quests as escapes from where we have been rather than as extensions of their location—we seek through our quests to outrun our past when the questions that come from it irretrievably tie us to it. And because we have seen our quests as escapes from ourselves and our past, we have failed to see the quest for what it is: a projection of our past into a new context. We have sought the overman by denying man rather than by allowing the inevitable to confront us, that man is always partially a result of what he has been, that our questing does not deliver us from our past but only reinforces its place in the future. Maturity would be the moment when we came to accept that our quests are heroic not because they seek to reject the past but because they accept the responsibility for it and seek to build a future on the basis of it. It is more heroic for the quester to bear his responsibility for the "It was" than to deny it, if for no other reason than this acceptance allows the quest to take a different shape.

The immature quester is seen as heroic precisely because he seeks to deny his past, and his heroism is the result of the fact that at the end of the quest he will always inevitably have to accept that which he sought to deny; he is a tragic hero because he fights against that which cannot be fought against, and he learns only that he cannot fight against it. The mature quester would be heroic because he began by accepting that which the immature quester cannot bear—his past—and sought to build his quest from there. The immature hero is more appealing because his existence is a denial of life and because his end is tragic; the mature hero seems less appealing because his life is based on the acceptance of the inevitable and because he is not defined by his end—it is not the end of his life that makes him heroic but the middle. We have come to prefer the immature quester only because we, like him, cannot bear our past. Indeed, we have so much difficulty bearing it that we are inclined to argue that one who accepts the "It was" must by definition have given up, for we cannot imagine a quest that is not based on a denial of the past.

In its own way, this is where so many interpretations of Nietzsche go wrong, for he seems like such a contradictory thinker that the only way we can deal with him is to reduce him to our own idea of the quest. When he talks about the will to power, we feel we are on safe ground, for we know what will is and what power is—for us, the will wills its own negation, it wills away the past, and the will to power is thus seen simply as the will's having enough power finally to eradicate the past. So when Nietzsche connects the will to power to the need to bear the thought of the eternal return and to accept the "It was," we become confused. After all, we see the will as our instrument of revulsion, not as the medium we should use against revulsion. We construe it as the instrument of revenge rather than a tool to be used against it, a means through which we can struggle against that which we cannot bear rather than as a tool that allows us to bear that which we are always seeking to escape. Nietzsche would have it otherwise; he would turn the will to power into a productive willing rather than a will to negate. He seeks a will that begins by bearing what it must and by willing the world out of its acceptance of what is. This seems such a strange use of the word "will" to us that we assume Nietzsche must indeed have been mad, for he is taking our one real instrument of power and denying its value for that over which we want to have power. And what good is a will that cannot will away what we want willed away? Far from speaking of the strength of man, then—in contrast to the weakness that Nietzsche saw in "Christian" man—we see Nietzsche's man as weak indeed, so weak that he accepts the one thing against which the will seems to be most powerful.

From Nietzsche's perspective, though, the strength of the will to power is not contradicted by bearing the idea of the eternal return and accepting time and the "It was." For Nietzsche, the sign of man's greatest weakness is his seeming inability to bear this burden, and if he has been fighting so strenuously against this weight for so long, the real mark of strength would be to accept it rather than reject it. The will to power is strong precisely because it wills itself to accept that against which man has so strongly been fighting, and because in bearing this acceptance, it wills life rather than death. If it is life against which man has been fighting, then the strength of the will does not come from fighting it but rather from fighting against the denial of it. And for Nietzsche this does not mean that man's quest has come to an end, but rather that he can finally begin to quest in a meaningful way only after he has ceased denying life—he can question without denying the consequences of his questions, he can question openly rather than seeking to put an end to inquiry.

What then would the quest for maturity and the maturity of the quest bring to man? On an individual level, it would lead to a considerable reorientation in attitude toward the events in one's life. One would have to begin with the assumption that there is no such thing as a personal quest, for one can no more frame such an itinerary than one can expect the world to submit to it. All quests, beginning with the questions that frame them, take place in contexts and within fields; all quests open up the world and in turn illuminate one's position within it, and for this reason the mature quest requires a consideration of the context of the question and the likely consequences of it. Too often human activity is discerned either in terms of its immediate impact or the long-term consequences, and the middle gets left out. To be sure, the middle remains, for what happens there generally causes one to readjust one's ideas of action to take account of what one's questions have brought to light. But we have become peculiarly inept at conceiving of the middle term of action. It is no accident that we all too easily tend to categorize people as either being devoted to immediate gratification or long-term, utopian goals that deny the present, yet we seem not to have a category for those people, the majority, who manage to live their lives in the middle without really knowing it. We have left the middle out of our systems of evaluation, and yet this is the terrain upon which the most crucial of all human actions takes place. A person supposedly devoted to immediate gratification nonetheless is usually forced to consider some middle-term course of action to generate the possibility of future gratification, and one with utopian goals must consider changes on the way to those goals if one is to have any hope of significant changes. But we have no methodology for the middle because it involves us in the acceptance of time in a way that immediate and long-term goals do not. The best we seem able to do in this regard is to argue that one ought to have long-term goals in order to generate significant effects in the middle term, a premise that is of value, but one that also inevitably subordinates the medium to the long term.

Another way of phrasing the problem is to say that we assume that life will take care of itself if we restrict ourselves to the short or the long range, and this is certainly true; but it is equally true that the goals of life are supposedly designed to enhance it, not to let it be lived in spite of one's goals. The most obvious example of this kind of thinking occurs in the domain of "career choices"—we are more or less brought up to think of these choices as the most important ones of our lives, the ones that will direct the flow of our lives from the moment of the choice onward, and this again is true. What career choices often fail to take into account, though, is the question of what things are most likely to enhance our lives and the life around us. This kind of question seems somehow hopelessly naïve, the kind one might raise in an ideal world, but certainly not one to put forward in our present societies. Yet without asking that question, and without investigating the context in which one asks it, the choices that end up being made are all too quixotic—they may end up well because we intuitively choose a series of directions that fit our contexts, or they may end up less fortunately because we fail to rely on any such criteria. Even if our societies assume that the best lives involve power, prestige, and money, it by no means follows that these things will enhance the lives of the majority of the people the way they are assumed to. They may or they may not, but they are certainly not universal criteria for a valuable life.

Because we do not consider the middle term in these kinds of decisions, we fail to ask ourselves what is most appropriate to our own context, and while we may eventually find a sense of appropriateness through "trial and error," we may also always fail to see what is appropriate by insisting on the validity of earlier choices in spite of evidence to the contrary. It is true that for millennia these were not crucial questions for most people because most of the decisions were beyond their control—their socioeconomic status determined what occupations they would have, as would their sex and race, and the other crucial aspects were heavily established as well. Until recently, most people did not conceive of an option to have or not to have children—they either did or they did not. We live at a time when choices are more available, yet we have failed to come up with ways of adequately questioning what is involved. To do so, again, would be to confront the middle of our lives, and we prefer to leave that as hazy and ill-defined as possible. Most of us prefer to be told what to do rather than to consider things for ourselves, first because it is easier, second because it diminishes our sense of responsibility, and third because it allows us to continue to avoid our revulsion against time. We choose to remain immature.

We seem to have arrived recently at a point where the possibilities of choice are once again restricting themselves for a whole series of socioeconomic reasons, but the range is still far greater than it was, and it is still far more than we are willing to deal with. Perhaps the most crucial change in the past century is the opening up of choice and possibility, yet we still remain terror-struck in front of it. Thus, we tend either to be immobilized by choices or find ways of getting others to make them for us. In between these possibilities seems to lie only boredom on a daily basis and the inertia of the repetition compulsion. One would almost think that the average human being was incapable of discerning in the least his capabilities or his needs when in fact the problem of choice involves responsibility, and that involves us in the "It was," from which we turn in fear.

In turning away from the notion of a personal quest and in focusing on the corporate nature of questions, one might think that one's responsibility is all the more awesome and terror-filled, for it extends all too obviously beyond oneself. To a certain extent this is true, though it has always been true in any case, and only man's conception of himself as a discrete unit was able partially to hide this from his gaze. More important, though, the mature quester sees that his main responsibility lies in what is opened up by the question and by his regular evaluation of that which continues to be opened up. The burden of this responsibility is not so awesome because it is regularly checked and changed according to the developments within the context the question opens up. The regular questioning of the question in the middle allows one periodically to adjust and alter those aspects of the initial query that seem not to be appropriate. One is free to open up new questions in terms of the responses one has gotten to earlier ones, so the chief responsibility is simply the determination to keep questioning and to keep the questioning appropriate to the context in which the queries occur. The change in the nature of the question of the middle is in part that it shows one and the world as emerging from the question rather than the other way around, and in part that the question is always only provisional, always only one possible vector through the middle out of the "It was."

In pragmatic terms, this means that one reverses the traditional direction of questions. The goal is not the end but the middle, and the question is a formulation of the middle rather than the end. One does not, say, ask oneself what kind of a career one ought to have and then formulate a program of action for achieving it; one asks what orientation one has, what conceivable directions it can lead to, and then formulates career questions as a pathway to test the validity of the direction and the orientation. The career is not the goal any more than it is a means to an end—it is simply a particular marker of a possible range of choices that one has decided to test, nothing more, nothing less. The more difficult aspect of this process comes not from obvious kinds of choices like that of a career, for they generally come after the already crucial choices have been made. The more important questions occur in daily life and the orientation one has to it—the way one marks or denies time through one's choices. The boredom quotient in daily life, for example, may well be higher today than ever before, and part of the increase is doubtless due to the reduction of most jobs to mechanical or near-mechanical activities; it may also well be due to the consumption model of society that feeds boredom so it can seemingly overcome it through consumption. Nevertheless, it cannot be said that these things were completely forced upon us; we also chose boredom and continue to do so. The social network may indeed suggest that work's primary value is to acquire money in order to purchase something, and that may indeed lead to the negation of vast segments of our days and the boredom that comes with the negation, but we are the ones who choose to believe that work should be negated in this way just as we are the ones who tend to extrapolate the boredom at work into boredom at home by making our leisure-time activities work as well. Likewise, one could say that our boredom is a result of the meaninglessness in our lives that society has foisted upon us, and this again may well be true to some extent, but we are the ones who continue to believe it and who regularly choose boredom over engaging activities. And we choose boredom not because we have no alternatives but rather because it is the only choice we can make that prevents us from having to consider our possibilities. The negation of time is the underlying principle of the world in which we live because we ourselves have desired to negate it, and if it turns out that we are unfortunately best capable of negating it through boredom—that state in which time stands still—we can still not avoid the fact that we arrived where we chose to go, only by a less pleasing route than we had planned on.

The question that opens out and leads through the middle is the converse of the question that focuses all the attention on the individual. If boredom is in a sense a state in which we are most truly ourselves inasmuch as we have focused all our attention on ourselves, then its most logical antidote is the open question that places one back in the world where one can mark out—rather than simply mark—time, where one can measure time through the action engendered by the question. The routine of life is overcome only by the openness of the question even as its openness depends on routine, for routine is nothing more than the locus of that which has worked and been understood fairly well while the openness of the question seeks continually to reopen the routine to new knowledge and new directions. The question that opens out opens up daily life and keeps it from settling into boredom because it provides an orientation to routine that does not force it back on itself but rather forces it to confront the world with which it is meant to deal. And because the open question is indeed open, it always leads to yet other queries that continue to frame the world one has chosen to live in and continue to change the life that is lived within the frame.

On an individual level, there is a clear distinction between the discursive and recursive modes of enframing, and it is the sense of enframing that generates the differences in orientation. The goal of the discursive frame is never to focus on the frame itself; rather, the object is to dissolve the frame altogether, to cut oneself loose from its constraints. From this view, the frame of a painting, for example, would be seen as a mark of the artificiality of the construct, for, after all, we know that in life things do not come framed, as they must on a canvas with limited space. Likewise, the discursive either tries to ignore that its questions are an enframing, or to argue that they are frames on the way to the end of all framing. The limit of the frame is always something to be overcome rather than to be investigated, something that gets in the way rather than a way of making something appear in the first place.

From the recursive point of view, no understanding is possible without a frame; the limited space of a painter's canvas is just a particular example of the limited frame of all human understanding and not an indication of mere artifice. All human vision is artifice in this sense, but that does not make it a purely artificial construct, for framing itself is an essential art of the natural world. But once one concedes the necessity of frames, one must also begin to consider their value as well. They can articulate different aspects of a context, so one is compelled to consider the different horizons they delimit and the particular value of each. The virtue of the discursive here is that by reducing the individual to an atomic unit, it made possible for a while the illusion that the individual himself was not such a frame, thus obviating us of the need to measure each unique frame. When it became clear that the individual was not isolated and discrete, the manner through which we framed things had to be investigated, a process still going on, albeit in a largely negative way. Inasmuch as limit does mean "illusory view" from within the discursive, investigations into those limits tend to stress the way our senses "distort" things. We are given studies that explain how the parallax of vision skews the way the real actually appears, as though there were a way of discerning what the real would be like outside of our "skewed" vision. We are presented views of the senses that are heavily binary, suggesting that they are connected to a computerlike brain that sorts the ones and the zeroes for us to point to the distinctive feature in any context with the idea that a "pure" vision would not have to be based on ones and zeroes. We have created large models of stimulus and response that seem to offer promise as they reduce our frames to tiny dots on a screen with the idea that these models will somehow help us eventually escape the fictions of our vision. So the perceptual mechanism continues from the discursive view to be seen in terms of a faulty machine that needs to be reprogrammed in order to make possible that vision that comes without a frame.

Of course we all know that our senses tend to pick out the distinctive features in any given context; after all, the new information in a situation is always construed as the most interesting and also potentially the most threatening. But why should this process be conceived of in a binary way? What is there in it that makes us think that distinctive features are isolated by sorting ones and zeroes? From the recursive perspective, this is what distorts the view of the frame, for it dissolves it into points on a plane rather than locations within a field, and the emphasis is generally placed on the foreground material rather than on the background out of which it emerges. We may not have pure vision, but we do always see things in a context before the features of the context emerge, and the recursive focuses on this process rather than on a sorting machine. Equally, it is not based on the view that this is a distorting process but sees it rather a revealing process that also conceals at the same time. The frame makes vision possible in the first place precisely because it is partial, but it also requires an investigation into the frame, that which is framed, and the orientation of the framing. The recursive is based on the view that the frame emerges from the world rather than being imposed upon it; we are in the world and in a context before we see ourselves so, and only by beginning from this perspective can we hope to arrive at an understanding of how frames come to emerge from the world out of which they develop. The frame is never called up arbitrarily but rather is called on to bring to the fore something of potential value. And because it is called up we need to pursue the manner in which it calls to us and why any particular frame was the one so called. It is inaccurate to say that a distinctive feature in a context called forth a particular frame, for a frame is needed to perceive a distinctive feature to begin with. Thus, we must assume that the context itself calls forth a frame that in turn orders certain elements in their relation to the overall context.

From the recursive view, we must come to see that which calls the frame forth before we can begin to get an idea of that which it frames and why it frames things the way that it does. Our inquiries and our language both suggest our relative ignorance of this calling of the frame, as the stimulus-response theory and the binary model of selection show. But our ignorance is even more obvious when it comes to things like personal relationships. We may we find ourselves attracted to certain kinds of people and wonder why this is so, for example, but we usually end up talking about such attractions in terms of particular characteristics rather than larger contexts. We speak of such attractions in terms of having things in common—we share an interest in ideas, or sports, or whatever. At the same time we come to realize over the years that we are not equally attracted to everyone who likes ideas or sports, and only some of them appeal to us. We might even go so far as to formulate the difference in orientation, saying that this particular person looks at sports as though it were played on the statistics sheet while we prefer the nuances and the rhythms of the game, or that another person treats ideas as little gems of wisdom to be stocked away while we see them as ways of confronting situations in everyday life. Having gone this far, we think we have understood the tracking mechanism of our frames, and the trial-and-error of our relations becomes more sophisticated.

From another, presumably more sophisticated, angle, we are told that the possibilities of attraction and repulsion are quickly played out in our earliest encounters with another individual, that our respective gestural languages are feeling out the possibilities in any situation long before we are even aware of it. And this is doubtless true, for we do first of all sort through the ways in which our responses to a given context might or might not correspond to another's just as we are equally perceiving such things as the space the person seeks to occupy and the manner in which he occupies it. But our investigations into these things have only begun recently, and the perspective—while it shows promise to the extent that it focuses on the manner in which people occupy positions within fields and the manner in which we probe their occupation—still generally reduces itself to "cues" and "gestures" rather than fields and frames that make sense of those cues and gestures.

From a more naïve perspective, we can see our ignorance in some of our uses of the word *fate.* After one has lived a certain amount of time, it usually becomes clear that one tends to be attracted to the same kinds of people over and over again, even when one thinks one is rejecting an earlier view of attraction. This is most obvious when it comes to relations we ultimately find less than appropriate. One may become married to a person who is ultimately violent and who abuses one and then divorce the person while looking for a better individual, moving on to someone who seems nice and gentle and the converse of what the previous person was like, only to find out later that the new individual is just as violent and abusive as the first one. Then one is inclined to tell oneself that one was taken in by the superficial qualities of the person, but if the same thing tends to happen over and over again, one begins to wonder if it is not simply one's fate to be attracted to violent individuals. The word *fate* in this context merely covers up our ignorance of what there is in us that attracts, and is attracted to, violent people. The result is that we never get around to pursuing the networks of attraction and repulsion upon which our actions are based; we do not investigate the contexts we seek out or the way we place ourselves in them, or even what we expect to get out of them. In part these things happen because humans can never be aware of all the variables in their lives—ignorance is to a certain extent inevitable. But a larger role is played by our naïve ideas of our own plasticity and by our credulous notions of how much we have control over the contexts of our lives. We see our decision-making processes as clear-cut—this kind of individual worked out badly, so I shall try to find his or her opposite—when in fact the crucial determinants of these decisions usually evade our grasp because we fail to see our-selves first of all in contexts and then investigate how and why we find ourselves in those contexts.

The problem we have in beginning from contexts is again our problem in dealing with that which has already been determined in our lives, with our history. Inasmuch as free will and determinism seem to be bound to the same binary network that most everything else appears to be, we see ourselves as having either one or the other but not both at the same time. We then fail to see how the two are inextricably connected and how one can learn to discern that over which one has free will only if one first learns something of the determinants in one's life. If we are the kind who regularly find ourselves in violent relationships, we might think about our past and conclude that we are attracted to such people because of the parental relationships we were involved in while we were growing up. Having arrived at that point, though, we would be likely to adopt one of two positions. We could conclude that we have free will and thus deny the effect of those relationships on us, a move that is ultimately bound to fail; or we could conclude that these influences on our behavior were so powerful that there is nothing we can do about them, that we shall simply have to resign ourselves to perpetually bad relationships. We seldom get to the point where we accept the power of our past over us while at the same time discerning exactly what power it has, how it precludes certain choices but still makes others possible. Thus, our understanding of our past does not help us to frame the possibilities that are open to us, nor does it help us understand how our framing of choices can help us alter the effect of our past on our present and future. This makes the past's effect on us a self-fulfilling prophecy, one from which we can seemingly never escape.

If we begin within the context, though, and with the situation of our own history, we can learn to see how our framing developed in the way it did, what is and is not valuable in our framings, and what can readily be changed in them. Only then can we begin to make estimates of value as to what things most need to be dealt with, what things are most worth expending ourselves on. Without arriving at this point, we are left either in the position regularly of rolling the Sisyphean boulder up the mountain or simply being crushed by it. Again, we are forced to find ourselves in the middle if we are to have any hope of arriving at the point where we can begin to understand our contexts, the frames that emerge from them, and our effects on those frames that mark out the meaningful in our lives.

The frame is a delimitation of value, and the values of any frame are in place long before we are aware of them. We find ourselves emerging through frames of value over which we seemingly have no control, and when we arrive at that knowledge we also find a feeling of helplessness toward the "It was" that is always irretrievably the "It was." Our sense of helplessness in turn encourages us to fight our knowledge in the hope that it will disappear. We will to ignorance rather than knowledge; we will negation rather than acceptance; and we thus will a yet stronger power of the "It was" over us. The vicious circle can only be broken by learning to bear the "It was" and by willingly accepting its eternal return, for only by accepting the eternal return can we learn to frame the "It was" in a positive way. The frame opens up a field and reveals to us the value it has and the value our relationship to it has, for we derive our own value in the world from the way we frame a field through our questions. We note this readily enough during conversations, where we are quite adept at discerning the values underlying certain kinds of questions and responses to others. It is relatively easy early on in a conversation to discern, for example, whether a person's questions are open or closed, whether they are designed to open up areas of inquiry or to stake out terrain for oneself, whether one considers the question or the questioner more important, whether one is more interested in seeing where a question goes or how it reflects back on the questioner, and so forth. And while we are busily working through these aspects of a conversation, we are also highlighting indirectly our own values, for we generally find more suitable the modes of questioning that are akin to our own, even if we are not fully aware of this at the time. One's values are always evident in the frame of one's questions, and we are quick to see this in others even as we tend to ignore the presence of our values in our own queries.

From the recursive perspective, most of the crucial value determinants occur along the lines above. A question that is designed to open up new terrain has a different value system than one that is designed to stake out one's turf, for example, for the second kind of question is really not a question at all. Instead, it is a mode of assertion designed to establish prominence. Its goal is thus not to open things up but rather to demarcate what is closed. The open question, on the other hand, shows a clear interest in the query itself, and the questioner shows a willingness to be led where it will go. Inasmuch as no questions are pure, they can be tinged with any number of motivations at the same time, but their general orientation is easy enough to discern, as are their values. Whereas there is no distinct barrier between the kind of question that focuses on the question itself and brings the conversationalists together and the kind that focuses on the question as a display of rhetorical virtuosity, the movement of the query usually indicates the orientation of it.

The central determinants of value are the questions of openness and orientation, whether the question comes from without or is designed to demonstrate the brilliance within, but these determinants manifest themselves in an infinite number of ways within individual contexts. It is also true that a question can be open without being recursive—the values embodied in a childlike curiosity about the workings of this or that object are open, but there is no conscious attempt to see the inquiry as part of a recursive series. The delight of the new seems enough on its own, and the desire to find the connections between different kinds of openness is lacking, meaning that the connections will either occur intuitively or not at all. A truly recursive question is always seen as part of a return that gathers it together with what has come before it, not only so that one can learn how to question better but also so that one can pursue new grafts between questions in the process.

The values of the frame begin with openness or closedness and then reveal the value in particular contexts. We are all located in the world in different ways, so our questions always reveal different aspects of our situation and the values we find embodied in the situations in which we participate. The quest underlying the frame of our values is in turn devoted to filling out our sense of situation at the same time that we try to expand the situation into other contexts. It is not simply that we choose to gain mastery over a field by being mastered by the questions with which it presents us, though that is of utmost importance and a worthy aspect of the quest; it is that we employ whatever we have mastered in one field in order to move into others, working from the relatively known terrain into an area of seeming compatibility about which we have an insufficient understanding. In this way, the quest is always moving us into new fields and allowing us to reconsider our understanding of that which we have already encountered. Our values grow and emerge further by the manner in which we employ our understanding in other fields and by the choice of fields in which to question and test our prior understanding. Mastery could be construed as the ability to broaden regularly the scope of one's understanding without denying the past out of which that sense of mastery developed. This is what prevents the recursive from being simply a trial-and-error process and what allows one more readily to build upon it.

If there were any significant stumbling blocks to an individual's development of recursive questioning, one of them would be the lack of understanding of direction and purpose. We are all taken up by open questions when we are caught up by the wonder of a moment or are struck by the strangeness of something, or in many other ways, but all too often people do not know what to do with such moments precisely because they seem so pointless. It may be well and good to feel for a moment the strange beauty of the world, if for no other reason than that it takes our mind off of our problems, as T. S. Eliot was fond of saying about poetry, but when the moment has passed, what can be done with it? What has been gained? A moment of relief perhaps and little more. And once open questions of this nature come to be seen as nothing more than this, their function is little more than the same one drugs have, and the question has the disadvantage of being unpredictable—one cannot necessarily call up the wonder of the question on command, whereas drugs will listen to us even if they too have their own commands. Because we live in a world that ultimately makes no distinction between the wonder of the open question and the thrill of a drug, we have lost much more than all those people who have committed their lives to drugs—we have lost in effect an entire mode of being. Open questions still exist, but in truncated form; they flit in and out of the mind without any sense of connection to one's life or to other areas of openness. Because our network does not even speak of these opennesses—we have entertainment instead—and because our schools have in the best of times only taught the recursive indirectly through the presentation of great human achievements, we are missing the idea that open questions are not only a positive and essential value in any culture, but also that one finally and essentially only builds a life out of them. So the glimmer of the question remains, but we no longer seem to know what to do with it.

At the same time, we are regularly presented with people who are capable of provoking wonder through their questions and generating much understanding as a result, but they are construed as doing something different than we do, as being so far superior to us that their minds must work in different ways. We may come to idolize an Einstein or a Joyce, but we reject our essential connection to them through our idolatry, which denies us a similar capacity to open up the world in new and interesting ways for ourselves and others. That is for great minds to do; that is their role in society, and in giving them that role and denying it for ourselves, we are cutting ourselves off from that which is most valuable in our lives, the questions that continually open the richness of life to our scrutiny.

Another aspect of the near loss of this mode of being is the simple fact that most people, even if they are attracted to the idea that the recursive opens the world to them in a new way, move away from it finally because it is too much work to practice such questioning. In one sense, this is an understandable reaction, for this mode of questioning is not generally encouraged at work, where it might obtrude on the smooth flow of production, and our leisure activities have become so easy that almost anything would seem like hard work in contrast to them. That our entertainments are also quickly boring seems less important than that they require minimum energy. These circumstances may indeed have something to do with why people may find the recursive hard work, but the more important reason for this reaction is simply that people have forgotten how easy it is and how intrinsic it is to human life. The open question is ultimately easier than the closed question, if for no other reason than that it always leads to yet another question, and the quest involved in such questioning provides more than enough energy and excitement to make one want to continue. The recursive is the easiest mode of activity in the world we know, though it does commit us to the discipline of the questions. It is also the only mode of questioning that allows us to make any kind of sense out of the strange interrelations of life at every level, and when it reaches a certain degree of sophistication, it seems to expand and grow of its own accord. But still it seems too difficult to be worth pursuing in our world. We gave up that mode when we passed out of the childhood ignorance of the medieval period and moved into the maturity of the Renaissance world, and we made that transition so long ago that we forgot what we lost just as we forgot that the medieval period was not exactly an age of childhood ignorance any more than it was the dark ages. The dark ages were really dark because the people of the time acknowledged the existence of darkness as the shadow of the light, and inasmuch as we no longer wish to confront the darkness, we need also to reject the openness of the question.

The values of the frame appear in many different guises, from the delimitation of hard work and easy work to the assessment of what and what not to spend time on, and in our everyday lives as well as within the larger social network, these are the most apparent determinants of our frames of value. The question is what we choose to spend time on and what we choose to work at, and it is all too easy to say that we seem finally not to want to spend time on anything, and we find nothing particularly worth working at. This would certainly be the view from the decadent critique of Western culture, but it ignores the fact that most people who see life in this way also seem to be incredibly disconcerted by what they see. Whereas the decadent school would see a valueless ethos, it is more obviously a crying out for values. People may well be confused about themselves, they may well be discontented with their lives, and the social network may have had a great deal to do with generating this confusion and discontentment, but this hardly shows a lack of values. What it demonstrates is a system where people have been trained not to see their choices as a reflection of value, where they have been given responsibility for their choices while being told that all of them are of equal value, where they have been told that enjoyment is something one pays to receive and work is something one goes through in order to enjoy. And it is not even that everyone actually believes these things, for most people go on living lives of value in spite of these ideas—their confusion is the result of the fact that the values in their lives do not correspond to what they expected, or rather, that there is no way to interpret their values within the social network because the recursive has been denied and put out of play, eliminating the mode of questioning that would give a sense of perspective to the values most people have yet do not know quite what to make of. Given the interpretive network of the discursive, their only alternatives seem to be to live within the confusion that so disorients them or else to return to a static system of values that forces their lives into a meaningful context—they can join a cult, for example, or commit themselves to IBM.

Even worse, part of the ethos that contributes to this malaise is the so-called revolutionary code, based in the Marxist dictum that one must first change the material conditions of life before one can alter the values of the society. Inasmuch as interpretations and modes of inquiry have nothing to do with the material conditions of life, and presumably nothing at all to do with action, they are merely retrograde or futile attempts to impose structure on people's lives from without. That the interpretation of life, the mode of inquiry, and the ethos involved in it have everything to do with changing the material conditions of life may or may not be apparent to such revolutionaries today, but even if it is, the rhetoric of action versus idea, material conditions versus interpretive network merely serves to reinforce the already existing situation.

The value of Marxian thought and of existentialist thought was that these concepts put an end to our naïve ideas of private action, to our belief that we could retreat from the larger world and live in our own. The problem, however, was that the Marxian system turned the social network into that into which the individual had to be absorbed while the existentialists sought to reduce everything to its point of origin in the individual. Inasmuch as neither provided an accurate view of the emergence of value and the individual in the world, though, both ended up reinforcing the importance of discursive thought, even though this was presumably that against which they fought. The first frame of value is man in the world, and value emerges from there through the questions that come to mark out the social/individual difference rather than the other way around. A child may well be exposed to the social system even before he is born, but his first location always situates him toward a world of which the social system is only a part and out of which his sense of individuality emerges while always remaining connected to the world from which that sense of self emerged. Even the adult who lives in a world saturated with social signs is first of all situated in the world out of which those signs emerged, and it is only because he is so located that he can properly distinguish the value of the social signs with which he is so regularly confronted. The ubiquity of the social network leads us to think that there is nothing else; indeed, most complaints about it center around the notion that the individual has been absorbed by it and has hence lost his meaning as a particular entity. In fact the individual has been reabsorbed into the world that he never really left, that he only seemed to have left through his assertion of individuality. The seeming omnipresence of the social system, then, has led us to the inevitable conclusion that it is not omnipresent, that it itself keeps being absorbed by the world around it just as it keeps bumping into the limits the world imposes on it; and it has brought us back to the point where we can see that it and the individual emerge from the earth rather than the other way around. We have yet adequately to realize the force of this recognition, but it has been pressing upon us with ever greater force.

The individual's questions, then, no more open up an individual space than they open up a purely social world; rather, they situate the social and individual with respect to the larger world out of which they arise. It is true that the social world limits the possibilities of questioning to a certain extent; indeed, at times it almost seems as though one's questions can only be formulated negatively—we can find where we do not want to go with our queries and yet seem incapable of moving beyond the negation of what is presented to us, but even if that were the only mode our questions could now take—and it is not—the aporias these questions lead to have their own effects, turning the values of the social network into voids that we refuse to follow. And even this belief is only the result of our conviction that society saturates everything—because we believe that, we see a void where in fact there is an openness. The result is that instead of exploring the openness, we continually point to the void and the question of openness closes in front of us; we continually point to the void and hope that someone else will take care of it. But both the question of the void and the question of openness are productive to the extent that they focus our attention on what is and is not capable of filling out the spaces that may seem empty. The question of the void, in other words, is really the question of openness—it is interpreted as void because it is a gap in the social network, and we assume that there is nothing other than the social network. When we discover that the socioeconomic world emerges from and remains connected to the earth, the question of the void is seen as the question of openness. Only our forgetfulness makes openness appear as void, but once it emerges as void, the possibility of openness once again comes to the fore as well. This is why thinkers like Nietzsche and Heidegger see themselves as occupying an openness while others see them as opening up the void— once the seam in the social network has been ripped open for everyone to see, those who see nothing but the social network begin to spy nihilists everywhere.

This is also why some of the best thinkers of our time have seen themselves as nihilists, as even Nietzsche did at times. They have accepted the inevitability of time and finitude, but their acceptance comes from a position that denies the possibility of anything other than social signs. The strength of their work comes from accepting finitude and opening up the world from that angle, but they are devoted to delineating the network of absences in the world because they assume that man is nothing other than a sign. Man *is* always only another sign, but he is also always other than his sign, and it is that distinction and the difference it embodies that generates the openness that is seen as void. While one may thus be dissatisfied with all the anthems to the void, the opening of the void that makes possible once again the reemergence of openness is the most important questioning that can be done. The only problem is that, ironically, those who praise the void do so in the guise of abandoning the traditional values that see the void as openness, when in fact the traditional values were based on the void and the negation of time rather than on openness.

For the particular individual, the problem of seeing the openness of the question as a void is that it leads him to think he has arrived at the negation of values rather than at the emergence of them, and in one sense this is true, for to arrive at the question of the void is to deny the value of the questions that have led one to it, and this could only be construed as the negation of values. But one was only capable of reaching the question of the void in the first place by allowing a different set of values to emerge through the process of questioning. What one has done, in other words, is negate one set of values through the values asserted by one's questions. Inasmuch as our thinking is interpreted discursively, we fail to make the return that would allow us to see the assertion of values of openness; the discursive moves along a straight line, so when one arrives at the void and its negation of values, one thinks that nothing is left but the void because one has failed to question the pathway that led one there in the first place. In making the return, one comes to see that the values of the recursive have been established in the process of negating the values of the discursive, and in making this return one is then able to see the void as an openness that allows new value to emerge in the place of that which is negated. To go no further than the negation is to remain locked within the discursive that one has already denied; to fail to see the assertion of the difference of the recursive in the negation of the discursive. Inasmuch as the original assertion of the discursive did the same thing—that is, it relegated the recursive to the void of chaos through the assertion of its own openness—we can see how easy it is to mistake the negation for an implementation of value, but once the return has been made, it becomes clear that the discursive itself is the opening into the void that makes the openness of the recursive possible once again.

Once the moment of negation has arrived in full force—and it has been upon us now for some time—one has only two options. One can continue to interpret the frame of one's values negatively, in terms of that center that has disappeared that would ground the values we once though we had, in which case all values are seen in terms of loss, in terms of what should have been or what we would have liked to be. Or one can begin to build on the values that allowed the void to appear in the first place, in which case all values come to be seen in terms of the possible, in terms of what can be achieved on the basis of what has already been accomplished, in terms of what the openness presents us with. In their own ways, both options work out into the openness, but the negative mode carries with it the heavy burden of nostalgia and revulsion along with its negations, so even though its opening is productive in the long run, the effects of its interpretive mode on the individual are more deleterious than necessary. Given the presence of the void/openness, then, it would seem preferable to probe the openness rather than increasing the void.

Looked at in terms of the psychological freight we bear as a matter of course, the values of openness can emerge in any number of ways, even though we have become more adept at the assertion of value through negation. We are masters of the anxious moment, the aporias of boredom, the never-ending sequence of disappointment and reversal; we have probed the interstices of these negative orientations like true devotees and pride ourselves on our ability to bear the pain we have engendered and so fully exploited. In each of these moments, there is an openness that is seen as a void, a possibility for the future that is instead seen as a negation of a past that never existed. In all of these anxieties and disappointments, however, is also the assertion of value through the belief in its absence. If we have become accustomed to asserting our values by lamenting their absence, though, and if we have come to cherish such apparently painful assertions of them, it by no means follows that this is the only way for our values to be made apparent. Anxiety, boredom, and disappointment are inevitable aspects of human nature, but they are not the only frames for value that we have available to us, even though they are effective. We make use of them simply because they are an essential aspect of the narcissism through which our values have come to be defined, but, like the discursive, there is no reason why they need to be the primary mode of thought through which we develop our values. They are always there to provide us with locations for areas of inquiry, and they should be used for that purpose, but openness manifests itself in positive ways as well, marking the threshold of possibility via our capabilities and potentiality and our rootedness in the world. To explore these possibilities at this point in history, we will have to accept the inevitability of the negative as well, something which we have always tried to avoid before, but this means no more than that at this point in history man is more capable than ever of making full use of that which he has available to him.

The frame of values is always a limit, a limit we have come to see as marked by the void and the negative, largely because it is always the limit we are trying to transcend, the boundary of time and finitude. For this reason, we have come to see the quest of the question as a heroic effort to leap over the limit, to move beyond the constraints imposed upon us by time and the earth. We have come to see the quest as a denial of limit and of time, even if that also means the denial of value and the closure of our openness to the world. The quest for an end to limit did succeed in opening up the possibilities of the world in many ways and did allow us fully to pursue the limits of that which was thought to be unlimited—discursive practice—but the value of this quest for us now begins with the fact that the discursive has moved to its limit, and in so doing has brought us back to the limits we sought to overcome. The return to the limit makes us see once again that the quest for the limit is the quest for return, the pursuit that opens up new terrain as it continues to frame the values that allow us to persist on the pathway that our questions open up for us. We have returned to our emergence as questioners through the emergence of the world we have questioned through the discursive, and now we are open to the possibilities of our joint emergence with the world in a different way. But before we fully establish ourselves on that pathway, we must redefine the nature of the quest in the question, and we must come to see the value in the limit, the threshold, the horizon that marks out our values. On an individual level, the orientation to the limit is clearly marked out, even if at times only through negation. On a larger level, the question is what this means for the world in which we should choose to live.

7 The Age of...

We live in a world that has been considerably transformed over the past three hundred years. Some would cite the great migrations to the cities, the greatly magnified industrialization, or the emergence of democratic and totalitarian systems of government as the major changes. Others would point to the development of the sciences and the new models for physics, chemistry, and biology that have led to great alterations in the way we think of the world in which we live and our capabilities to change it. Still others would point to the technology that has evolved from our sciences, most particularly the growth of the computer industry and the information-processing systems that derive from it. All of these changes are interrelated, of course, and it is difficult to separate the effects of one from the others; it is also difficult to discern how these changes have affected man and his own sense of himself within the scheme of things that he has in part created. Our philosophers have told us about alienation, depersonalization, dehumanization, and the like, and out of those ideas have come images of man with total freedom, in more or less total bondage, or as merely one signifier among all the others in language. Man's powers have been asserted at the same time that man has also been dissolved into nothing more than a mark on the page. And for the most part, little of what has been said about man in this world has seemed pleasing to most—either it has given humans so much responsibility for their actions that they cannot bear the thought of taking it up, or it has atomized them to the point where there seems no room left for a concept of the human at all, much less a concept of responsibility. In general, our theories have derived from the discursive and have thus focused on the void that man faces, the void that in a way he himself is.

Along with these new views of man has come an ever-increasing sense of impending doom—our thoughts have more and more turned toward the apocalyptic, a tendency that was given greater force with the introduction of nuclear energy into the world, but one that was quite strong well before that event occurred. We are so used to living with this sense of impending doom that it almost seems second nature to us now, and it certainly is, for man has always had the apocalyptic tendency more or less at his side. If it has always been there, though, this does not mean that we should necessarily ignore it. As Milan Kundera has said, something that has been so omnipresent must certainly have some truth to it, so it is worth attending to for that reason alone. There are also glorifyingly optimistic scenarios about the future of our species, depicting an age in which we will have all the information we need at our fingertips, when robots will perform the unpalatable tasks that need to be done, when we understand the way cells work and disease and aging have been eliminated, when we have come to understand the nature of the universe, and so forth. And it is not surprising that both the positive and the negative scenarios rely pretty much on the same phenomena—they focus on science, technology, information, demography, and so on, but one sees these things as marks of great potential while the other sees them as instruments of our own demise.

The surprising thing is not that the positive and negative views of the future make use of the same materials; it is rather that both depend upon a view of man and the components of his civilization that is more than three hundred years old. The difference in view is merely a change in emphasis that is based on a belief in man's capabilities—those who see great possibilities emphasize man's potential power and his ability to control that which he has allowed to emerge; those who despair see man as a slave of his own inventions, powerless to control them, yet powerless to have done with them as well. In both cases, man is still seen as opposed to the earth, and in the one case opposed to his own knowledge of the earth, so our view of man in the face of the future reflects the man who emerged in the Renaissance before all the transfor-

mations of the Renaissance fully developed. And if man himself has changed through that which he has come to understand in the past three centuries—a change not so much in
"human nature" but rather in the understanding of where it
fits into the world of which it is a part—then we must begin
to reconsider his position and his future on the basis of that
change.

The process of redefining man and his situation in this way
has been going on for some time now, but the view of him
that has begun to emerge has yet to be adequately turned back
upon the world of his transformations. Nietzsche suggested a
shift in man, but his goals did not lead him to address specifically the world in which man lived. Heidegger turned to the
effects of science and technology to demarcate the new and
the older senses of man, but the chief burden of his work was
directed toward the negative consequences of perpetuating
the older view. Those who have chosen more specifically to
confront the facts of human existence have generally focused
on the repression of governments and the limits of human
freedom within the social networks, and they only address
the more obvious facts of science and technology when they
seem to contribute to man's repression of man. What is also
needed, however, is some idea of how our changing conception of man affects our attitude toward human equipment,
an idea that does not begin from the assumption that the
equipment is inherently destructive or beneficial. What is
required is a view of how that equipment has helped to situate
man, and how man has come to situate his equipment.

Any discussion of man and his tools should begin by asserting that man's control over his tools is no more dominant
than the control of these tools over man. We tend either to
see our equipment as having taken over from us—hence our
horror at our powerlessness—or to see ourselves as still controlling it as we see fit, and both views are clearly naïve.
Our horror at the prospect of our tools' controlling us—seen
regularly in science fiction for some time now—shows that
we have come to see that our tools affect us and are not value
free, that we do not have the control over them we thought.
Because we mistakenly assumed we had control, we over-

reacted when we found this not to be the case and came to fear what our tools could do to us. Now that we have seen the necessary interrelations between tools and man, though, there is no reason for us to consider the relation between the two simply in terms of crude power dynamics.

If we imagine a time when man first developed the necessary tools to plow the land, we can perhaps get some idea of the variables involved. The traditional way of looking at this moment is that the invention of tools to plow the land—or rather the invention of the idea of plowing—allowed man greater control over his immediate circumstances. Because he was able regularly to cultivate one plot of land, he could discontinue his nomadic way of life. Instead of having to move on every time his food supply was depleted, he could remain more or less in the same place, perform certain regular activities, and guarantee himself a sufficient food supply without having to move on. This power over the land was limited by pestilence, plague, drought, and the like, which could on their own force man to move on once again, but still there was a greater stability in his life because of the invention of cultivation and a greater power over circumstances as well. In the traditional view, this moment was one of mankind's greatest steps forward, and no doubt it was.

From another angle of vision, however, we can see how the invention of the tools of cultivation commanded a certain amount of power over man. Inasmuch as the benefits of cultivation seemed so obvious—a greater guarantee of food supply, less of a need to be transient, a greater sense of security—the losses involved in the transaction were doubtless not considered. The presence of the tools of cultivation, their specific reality, so framed the possibilities of the future that they had to be made use of. They held out great promise, and man doubtless turned to them without fully realizing the consequences. It is difficult to imagine the man who invented the tools of cultivation getting too much beyond the vision of a guaranteed food supply and the elimination of the need constantly to be on the move. It is equally difficult to imagine him considering whether he was better suited to the life of a nomad or a farmer, weighing in turn the advantages and disadvantages of each, particularly when he had probably not yet become aware of many of the disadvantages of cultivation. Inasmuch as he had not cultivated land over any period of time, it would be difficult for him to know all of the things that could go wrong, and inasmuch as he was not accustomed to returning to familiar places, or remaining in one place all the time—even if his nomadic route did bring him back to the same places over the years—he was not likely to know of the limitations inherent in remaining in one place.

Likewise, inasmuch as the transition to cultivation was doubtless not immediate but gradual, man probably did not know how much the circumstances of his life would change as a result. And in one sense the failure to consider these things increased the power of the tools of cultivation over him, for by the time he had learned enough of the circumstances of cultivation he was committed to the tools in a way that would preclude their easy abandonment. If the idea of the tools had power over him because of the positive prospects for change they might introduce, the tools themselves were even more powerful because they inaugurated certain rhythms in man's life that quickly altered the measure of his old ways—they transformed his attitude toward himself and toward the world in which he lived.

From yet another angle, we could investigate the relations of power and control as they changed with the introduction of the tools of cultivation in a more complex way, beginning with the assumption that the idea of power and control first gained a strong foothold in the mind of man here, for this marked the moment when he asserted a degree of control over the natural processes around him. As a hunter-gatherer, he was dependent on what there was available to hunt or gather; he picked up what was available, and if his search was no longer random because he had found locations that were more likely to have something worth hunting or gathering, yet he still had to depend on the appearance of food outside of his control, even if he thought he had magic to conjure it up through various symbolic means. The invention of tools for cultivation gave him a power that mere tools of the kill did not, and if he became enslaved to certain rhythms of life that came along with the tools, that was a worthwhile trade-off. The tools altered the network of relations between man and nature by allowing man to assert a greater priority over nature and formed a triangular bond among man, tool, and earth that created new limits and possibilities, even if they had yet to be learned and fully framed. Man could imagine greater power over nature only by distributing some of nature's power to the tool, which was in turn able to exercise certain power over nature and also over man. This redistribution of power relations appeared to be to man's advantage, though he probably did not see how the tool commanded power as well. He would learn that as he watched the alterations it introduced.

The potential changes in power introduced by the tools of cultivation seemed to increase the quotient of power itself. Man had greater control over nature, and the tool had some control over both man and nature, yet it could not be argued that this power was taken away from nature, for it too had greater power. Not only was the earth capable of producing more, but the reserve power nature had over man increased as well—his fixed location made him more dependent on the natural processes that affected that location, even more so when his dependency reinforced his forgetfulness of other, earlier options. And abstractly, while man asserted greater power over natural space by remaining in a fixed location, thus denying the rhythm of return he had as a hunter-gatherer, the space of the point of tool and location did not remove him from the rhythms of the seasons that were behind the patterns of hunting and gathering to begin with. Indeed, the idea of the space of the point made his dependence greater because it focused his attention on one location to the exclusion of its participation in the larger rhythms around it; the point of the tool of cultivation focused the point of space, which in turn focused the point of man, each one intersecting and redefining the other, each in a sense giving greater power, each in a sense becoming more fragile as well by being reduced to a point rather than a location within a field of play.

At this juncture we begin to see how the idea of relations of power—compelling though it is—has less and less applicability for evaluating what has changed with the introduction of the tools of cultivation, for the power that is established also creates a network of dependency that generates its own, albeit different, kinds of fragility. Perhaps, then, we need to move away from the mark of the point that was introduced with the tools of cultivation and return to the scene of cultivation in terms of the limits, horizons, and thresholds that it established in order to discern how those were altered by the introduction of the tool. Most obviously, the tools of cultivation gave man a greater understanding of the limits of nature at the same time that those limits were expanded. In introducing regularity to the growth of some plants, man was able to discern more of the elements that were involved in the production of plant life and was equally able to increase plant production in a local way by carefully tending one location rather than simply making use of what was available. The limits to the process of cultivation were doubtless not all immediately apparent; the requirements of water and the like were easy enough to establish, but a certain amount of repeatability was necessary to learn that the same plants year after year come to generate less of a yield, and the changes in other plant and animal life in the area of cultivation were even more difficult to read. In expanding the limits of natural growth in a local way, though, man did open up more natural possibilities at the same time that he was able to push them to the limit and discern what boundaries there were when it came to local changes in the natural network.

In so discerning the limits of the process he had opened up, he was also able to extend his own limits by guaranteeing a regular, seemingly stable food supply and by registering a certain degree of control over the process. When the limits of the process began to emerge in lower yields, or whatever, he could always move on with his tools, but the need to be on the move regularly was eliminated. In turn, the process of cultivation made man's security needs different and allowed him to deal with them better because he could provide a stable location of defense—he might have to confront more seriously the species whose terrain he had permanently invaded, but he could also sufficiently establish himself on the terrain better to ensure his safety. This and the greater certitude of food supply also made it possible for him to live in greater numbers and to produce more of the species, which would also further enhance his security in the long run, even if it equally increased his vulnerability to the viscissitudes of crop production. Finally, there was doubtless a shift in the level and kind of skills man put to use through cultivation, minimizing the capabilities that were needed for regular travel, for example, while enhancing those that depended on learning from regularly repeatable experiences and extending his understanding of the effects of seasons and the like on the world in which he lived. The tool, in other words, in allowing man to remain in the same place, both suggested a cleavage between man and his world and made understanding more possible by creating an environment that could be regularly investigated for its changes and the consequences of them. In narrowing the horizon of the world to a local plot of ground, the tool expanded the possibilities of understanding the complex network of relations that took place within that plot.

The tool in its turn became not merely an instrument for the manipulation of soil but the locus of an entirely different relationship between man and his world. Because it focused things, because it pointed to a moment of relation that expanded outward, the tool gave man a location through which to measure his world, and in so doing opened up its own potentiality as well. Its functions were limited to those which man sought to make use of, but it had the ingenious capability of being expanded almost infinitely through the introduction of other tools, each of which altered the tool's possibilities, each of which changed the relationship it had initially established. The tool was thus capable of expanding its own limits at the same time that it inevitably opened up nature and allowed man further to address the thresholds of his own capabilities. As with both man and nature, though, the tool also brought along with it its limits—if for man it altered his sense of space and time by focusing on a point, if for nature it changed the network of local relations by making possible the cultivation of one particular location, its own value was measured as the interface between the new network of relations between man and nature. It could only be put to use by man, and it could only be applied to certain limited circumstances, even if they were expandable—a tool for cultivation could also be used as a weapon, or it could be used for digging for water, but it might not work in splitting rock. The tool worked precisely because it did have limits, because it was capable of focusing relations in a specific way, and while its limits, like man's and nature's, were expandable, they were not infinitely expandable.

Now the introduction of the tools of cultivation doubtless did not bear all of this freight in any obvious way when they first appeared, and the matter was doubtless not as simple as this; certainly language is involved in this process in some way, and certainly the changes that were introduced by cultivation led to other alterations, as when the tools were not simply taken from what was at hand but were crafted by man, when he discerned the capabilities of metallurgy and the like. But the triangular relationship among nature, tools, and man nevertheless bears a composition akin to the one I have outlined, and it is more or less the same relationship that we have today, even if the transformations of the earth have proceeded at a great rate over the intervening millennia. And in a real way we are only now beginning to understand fully the changes that were introduced with the tool, even if we are still reluctant to consider the consequences of what we have come to know. We have come to see that the crucial aspect of the tool is its point of focus, its way of delineating the relationship between man and nature in terms of a specific context. Likewise, we have come to see that the focal point of the tool radically altered man's sense of space and time; we see, in other words, that the tool in our minds is inextricably combined with our idea of transcending space and time, for it was the device through which we came to the notion that we can have some degree of control over them. In focusing the world to a local space, the tool provided man with the capability to have a greater effect on a particular space, which in turn gave man the idea that he could control the local space for his own purposes. To be sure, every local space had some limits built into it, but when confronted with the limits, man was often ingeniously capable of dealing with them, which at least provided the possibility of ultimately overcoming the limit. And because the local space was focused by the tool, the tool allowed man to think of his space as something separable from the earth; after all, he no longer had to devote himself to the rhythms of hunting or gathering, a process that defined space as an intricate network of interrelations within fields, so he was able to imagine his own cultivated space as different from the tracts of land over which he previously had to roam. In so focusing the local space, the tool was able to give man the idea that the limits of locality were intrinsic to the locale and not a part of that network of interrelations in which he participated as a hunter-gatherer. He defined the limits in terms of the isolated space and not in terms of the larger network, and inasmuch as he was able to deal with some of those limits by so conceiving of the space, he was encouraged to forget the larger network of which the space was a part. The focal point of the tool allowed man to conceive of the local space as separable from the environment around it, just as it allowed him to think of himself as separable; after all, he was no longer following the rhythms of the larger terrain; he had focused himself on a specific piece of ground, isolating himself as well as the land, focusing on himself as different from those other creatures who were an intrinsic part of the rhythms he himself had escaped through the tool.

Similarly, in so focusing space to a point, the tool focused time. In remaining in one place, man was able to imagine himself as outside of the rhythms he previously participated in. True, the crops themselves depended on them, but man was now capable of seeing himself as an observer of the rhythms rather than as a part of them. He remained in place and learned how the rhythms of cultivation functioned; he marked time by the processes of his cultivation rather than by his movements on the earth—everything else moved, but man remained in place, which led him to achieve a much greater understanding of the movement of the earth, but which also made it possible for him to think that he was the only thing not participating in those movements. He could conceive of time as the measurement of the distance between two points, and inasmuch as he was the point that did not move, he could imagine being outside of time because he could see how he was previously in time. In order to survive as a point in space, man still had to respond to the same rhythms of time and space that he participated in before, but he was able to think of them differently, just as he was able to conceive of his own rhythms as differing from them. Because his point of focus made these changes possible, however, and because the horizon of the point of focus was forgotten, man was able to work quite well with this new sense of space and time, if for no other reason than when something went wrong, he could move elsewhere and establish another point of view.

One result of the focal point of the tool, then, was that through a different conception of his place in the world, man was able more or less to forget about his earlier sense of space and time, so long as he instinctively adhered to its laws. Whereas the rhythms of hunting and gathering had once been in the foreground, interrupted by local effects that were attended to but never identified as anything other than effects in the larger rhythm of things, man was now able to place the larger rhythm in the background and to situate the point of space and time in the foreground, and he could mark his difference from those rhythms precisely by focusing space and time through the point of the tool. This is basically the way man in the West still functions today, even if he has become more and more aware of the rhythms that were placed in the background and forgotten. The problem is that even though those rhythms have emerged with more and more insistence, we are so used to seeing our lives in terms of the point that we do not know quite what to do when we are confronted by them. Even more, we do not really wish to deal with them and do our best to avoid the problem altogether. Avoidance is easier in some areas than in others, fortunately, and even better, because we are accustomed to the point and the line, we can see the problem of the larger rhythms as isolated cases and then take on the ones that are easier to deal with. Thus, writers like Nietzsche and Heidegger can be seen as simple examples of a certain kind of decadence that has crept into our culture, but they are no more important than that. They are certainly writers whose ideas must be put out of play, but they deal, after all, only in ideas, and those are fairly easily put on the shelf, particularly when they seem threatening. Other ideas, more prominent perhaps and more obviously affecting our lives, like the theory of relativity and the new physics, do not really need to be dealt with at all because they are too obscure for most people to understand, and while they may have changed greatly the world in which we live, there is no reason why we need recognize them in our daily lives as the assertion of these background rhythms we have done our best to forget about. Physics is likewise an isolated case, so there is no need to assume that what has happened within that discipline has anything to do with us.

There are, to be sure, other domains in which the background rhythm has asserted itself, most obviously on the everyday level in terms of pollution, but we have cleaned up our smokestacks fairly well and can occasionally see the horizon again, so that problem—again an isolated one—is being attended to well enough by the expert. More serious kinds of pollution, chemical and nuclear wastes, have not been sufficiently dealt with, largely because no one knows quite what to do with them, but they are not obtrusive on our daily lives, and in any case, our native ingenuity and our tools will help us come up with a solution sooner or later. And these, too, are isolated by-products of local events, so there is no reason to see them as part of the same larger rhythms that control other crucial aspects of our lives. Crop yields too are another isolated case—the soil may be disappearing at a rapid rate, but we have had one green revolution already, so there will doubtless be another one before all the topsoil blows away or is covered up by tract houses. Water supply—well, that is problematic in some areas, but we can always find more water elsewhere and bring it to where it is needed; we can reverse some rivers or get into the business of towing icebergs to where water is in short supply. The increasing amount of desert space in the world? Like water, an isolated problem generally caused by the ignorance of people who do not know how properly to cultivate land in this modern age.

Of course, there are those who argue that these are not isolated phenomena but all part of the larger reassertion of the background rhythm we have chosen to forget in our assertion of the point and the line, but even if they are part of a larger rhythm, we shall be able to deal with them indirectly as points on a line without considering their connection to other phenomena. We have all become environmentalists when we need to be.

Even if these natural problems we are facing are part of the reassertion of that background rhythm, though, it is more speculative to take the step into cultural affairs and argue that they too are affected by the increasing obviousness of this rhythm. We hesitate to do this first because we consider culture to be different from nature rather than a part of it, even if we concede that our tools do come from nature and even if we admit our own connection to nature. Equally, there is no doubt that a great many of our problems are the result of flaws in our governmental and economic systems that have nothing in particular to do with the reassertion of the rhythms of the earth. We are nevertheless aware of the depletion of minerals and energy sources just as we know of the depletion of water tables and arable land, and while there is no doubt that the ingenuity of man can overcome the problems at least temporarily—and perhaps for a considerable time—there is also no doubt that sooner or later the issue of the use of these resources, and the limits to their use, will have to be confronted. None of these problems is necessarily an immediately crucial factor in our lives, but the regularity with which such difficulties are beginning to recur should at least suggest to us that it is time we listened to the rhythms we have forgotten about.

The use of resources is probably best confronted through that system we call capitalism, for, efficient as it is in one regard, it is very inefficient in its exploitation of resources. We are told that a central premise of our economy is its need to expand. Indeed, we are told that its need to expand is directly connected to the stability of our democratic forms of government—without the possibility of an increasing share of the wealth for everyone, someone will have to determine what goes to whom, who shall get less and who shall get more. To be sure, governments perform this activity as a matter of course, but the situation changes when the economic "pie" is no longer expanding. We apparently thus face a very strong argument for the need for our economies to expand, even if that means that the way in which they expand is less important to us than that they do in fact expand.

On the other hand, the economic world is facing a series of limits that are similar to the ones we find in other areas. Most of the globe is covered with people, and most of the people on the globe prefer not to have their own wealth exported for someone else's use without proper payment. Just as we could ignore the changes that were introduced in the cultivation of a plot of ground so long as it was only one plot of ground, so too we could ignore the other voices in the world when they were not sufficiently aware of what was being done to them— we could believe that we were not increasing our own wealth at the expense of others simply because we evaluated the world in terms of our own plot of ground. But just as when most of the available cropland has been tilled and we begin to see the limits in the possibility of tilling—and the consequences involved in tilling all the land we can—so too when it is no longer possible to see one's economic plot of ground extrinsic from the other economies that have asserted themselves, it then becomes difficult to see the infinite expansion of wealth as a real possibility. Likewise, when one has the only market for a commodity, one can see the world differently than one can if one's commodity must face competition from a number of other sources. Faced with this situation, there are still ways of expanding productivity and thus increasing the available wealth, but the limits of wealth also become apparent, and they are not infinitely expandable.

When such a scenario arises, we may begin to encounter treatises like *The Limits to Growth* and *The Zero-Sum Game* that seek to deal with these economic problems, but, knowing as we do that there is at least some correlation between an expanding supply of wealth and a stable democratic process, we may well choose to believe in the infinite expansion of wealth. Inasmuch as the limits to such possibilities have only begun to become clear relatively recently, we may not face any imminent crisis if we continue to believe in the infinite expansion of the line. There are still enough resources and markets and innovations to postpone for some time dealing with the background rhythm of which these limits are a part. Indeed, it may well be that no one now living will necessarily confront the full force of these limits, even if they do encroach more and more on our lives. The point is not that we face a necessarily imminent crisis of limits—though that too is a possibility—but that we have arrived at a sufficient understanding of the world to know that the background rhythm of limit that we had forgotten is still there, and that, knowing of its existence and finding it reassert itself in so many different domains, we are forced to connect the point and the line back into the rhythm of the return that is increasingly hard to ignore.

Within the cultural and the economic worlds it is difficult at this point to know how much of the reappearance of the background rhythm is the reassertion of the natural rhythm inherent in culture and how much these systems simply have similar limits built into them, as they surely must inasmuch as one cannot finally separate the cultural from the natural. The limits to resources and the like are clearly natural barriers within the cultural, while the limits to cultural activity when most of the cultures are fully aware of each other doubtless have something to do with the limits of the human—a natural limit—and something to do with the relationships between particular cultures—a limit that derives from the location of the culture within the world but which is also dependent on more clearly mediated functions like language. Governmental and economic systems are derived in one way or another from local expression yet remain dependent upon their larger relationship to the earth for their overall effectiveness. Investigations into these matters are at present hazy at best, largely because the invention of the point and the line led us to imagine a culture that is separate and different from the natural world out of which it emerged, but the fact that there is no such thing as an unmediated view of the natural processes of the world also complicates these issues.

It is possible to argue that all of the phenomena I have mentioned are indeed discrete and unrelated—that is, after all, one of the values of the line—and at the very least there is no doubt that not all of these limits have reached the same degree of saturation for us—some are more obvious than others, some more compelling than others. But if a new perspective of our positions in the world has emerged in the past hundred years or so, it seems to have applicability over a wide range of phenomena, so it seems worthwhile to explore the possibility of the interrelatedness of these limits. Indeed, we have already been doing this for some time—we have simply approached those limits in terms of the void, of the negation of what we have thought, of the denial of our previous views of the world. From the point of view of the line, limit always comes to be defined negatively as that which impedes or denies man's will even as man wills to deny limit. As with the individual, though, we have just begun to think of the limits of the background rhythm as marks of potential rather than as a denial of possibilities.

To discern the potential in the limit, we must first redefine the relationship among man, his culture, and nature—each limits and defines the other in ways that cannot be avoided, regardless of our attempts to imagine culture as that wedge of opposition against nature through which we could conquer it. The difference between the two is what allows man to emerge in the first place, and the manner in which man continues to emerge develops and further defines the differential, but, as with all differences, the threshold between the two is not a nonpermeable membrane—there is transference in each direction as each helps the other further to elaborate itself through its difference. Man is the by-product of this emerging differential rather than its point; he is the difference that is worked out through their difference rather than the other way around—and only by seeing the difference and man's relation to it can we understand the rhythms that regularly define the differential of nature and culture.

In the practical maintenance of our affairs, we have always seen the culture/nature difference as that which allows men to emerge, but because we have failed to interpret our activities in this way—choosing instead to place ourselves in the foreground—we have failed to learn from that which we have helped generate. Because culture always begins before we do, we have been quite willing to slip into its stream and work out of it, yet we have chosen not to see ourselves in that light because it seems demeaning to our sense of individuality. Instead of seeing our difference as emerging out of our location within the culture/nature differential, we have seen ourselves as asserting our individuality over against culture and nature; the result has been a working against the grain of that which most readily allows us to be what we are. But the real danger in that view is not that a particular individual sees himself this way but that we have come to define our cultures in that light. The result is that we as individuals and as a culture have come arbitrarily to assert our priority over culture and nature and so have squandered our own energies—if the primary value of an action is the assertion of priority over culture and/or nature, which it has increasingly become, then it makes little difference what the precise action is so long as it generates the appearance of priority. From this viewpoint, the invention of the computer has the same value as the assassination of the most prominent world leader. The problems inherent in this view are most obvious through that example, but they are more pernicious within the vast middle ground between those extremes, for that is where the majority of human actions take place, and that, therefore, is where this skewed idea of values has its greatest effects, in the countless actions that are considered only for their ability to assert one's priority over difference. The corollary to this facile assertion of priority within our culture, though, is equally problematic, for those who do not see their actions in terms of that standard are still not presented with a viable alternative, which means that the values that go into their actions are not well considered either inasmuch as they find no ready gauge by which to consider them.

The priority of culture over man, through its differential relationship with nature, must be our beginning point. To establish in a general way the obviousness of this premise, one need only look at the kinds of demographic shifts that we have become increasingly adept at tracing. As we made the move to urban cultures, for example, most people did not consider the issues involved in moving to the city or remaining behind in the country in terms of the effects such a shift would have on them or the culture at large. Perhaps the notion of "opportunity" drew many to the cities, while others merely came as a result of the pull of the culture in that direction, while still others came as a result of the lack of sustenance in the country, but certainly on the whole the culture provided the opening for the shift. Likewise today, at a time when people are moving away in some numbers from the city, each for his own reasons, each perhaps convinced of the assertion of his priority through this choice, who really considers his action in terms of the shifts within the cultural network that encouraged him to make such a move? Does each individual choose these shifts for himself? In part, no doubt, yet the reasons behind them are always generated by the larger cultural network—the job opportunities are elsewhere, or the climate is better, or whatever. And there is no denying that job opportunities have a great deal to do with cultural changes, but who determines where the job opportunities will be? Natural resources play a part—if oil is a valuable commodity, people are drawn to places where it is found. Cultural differences play a part, as reflected in a variety of things ranging from tax codes to ways of life. But who determines when one thing becomes more valuable than another? Who finally decides that, say, a better tax shelter is more valuable than a better transportation network? And the situation is even more obvious when it comes to things like climate. If more and more people in the United States are moving to warmer regions, who was it that decided that warmth was now more valuable than a higher wage? The warmer parts of the country were there long before they became the place to move to, and the northern regions have not gotten any colder in the meantime. To be sure, the presence of air conditioning makes the rather hostile summers in the South more bearable, but how does one decide whether it is a good trade-off to move to the South—and live in conditions more artificial more of the time than they are in the North—than to remain where one is?

If we are moving from urban areas to less urban areas, how did we decide that the price of living in an urban environment, with its congestion, crime and the like, was not worth it any longer, that it was preferable to live more comfortably with the inconveniences posed by living outside of the city? One could say that we have come to define our standards of living differently, that money has come to mean less to us than the overall quality of our lives, but that begs the question as well, for it requires the determination of value of one quality of life over another, which is precisely what is at issue. These movements are occurring at a time when we have become more sophisticated at charting them, so they may not seem so readily to demonstrate culture's priority over man, but they do suggest how complex these movements are, how little we know about them, about how they come about, how our choices are related to these larger movements, and how we are to go about evaluating our position with respect to them.

One other example of this kind would be the question of who works at what within a culture and how many hours are worked. At least until recently, no one gave much thought to the number of hours each day that should be devoted to work, yet over the millennia the time required of man to sustain his existence has varied a great deal, from a relatively few hours a day to twelve, fourteen, and more. If we have now established for the time being that eight hours a day seems an appropriate figure, and if we have come to think of our lives as necessarily connected to eight hours of work a day, this figure is based more on our memory of how long some people used to work than on how few hours were once required for the maintenance of human life. Similarly, the great influx of women into the economy over the past generation was not something that we or our government thought out ahead of time any more than we contemplated the changes it would bring to the entire social network, from the family to the economic output of the country to the problem of unemployment to the increasing strength of the women's movement.

None of these things simply happens—there are always a great many factors that go into such shifts—but in spite of being carried along by such shifts without ever being even halfway aware of them until they have already taken place, we choose to see our actions as having priority over the emergence of the culture itself.

The same situation is apparent in the development of our technologies. We should prefer, for example, to imagine that such things as the computer were invented by one or more people who then began to establish uses for them. But it is at least as useful to believe that the computer was invented because certain questions were asked on the path of emergence of the culture/nature differential—the differential between the two had generated an understanding of the cultural and natural networks that was sufficient to allow this technology to emerge, and once it appeared, it increasingly came to be seen as one of the important determinants in the differential itself, making available, as it did, the tremendous expansion of information relevant to that differential. Having arrived at the emergence of this technology, we could then either say that the innate flexibility and capacities of man made him see what cultural and natural transformations could be generated by this new technology, or we could say that the emergence of the technology itself was the result of a shift in the differential that allowed an openness into which the technology naturally fit. And inasmuch as in many ways man seems not to have been fully ready for this technology, and in many ways still does not seem ready for it, resisting and fearing it as he does in so many respects, it would seem more likely that it was the openness of the culture within its differential with nature that was the crucial element in the emergence and swift transformation brought about by the "invention" of the computer.

To be sure, such a description depends upon an attitude toward culture that is not conventional, first, because it asserts that man is the by-product of the differential rather than the generator of culture in opposition to nature; second, because, as a result, culture is not seen as an aggregate of humans bonded together by the history of a particular location but rather as the history of a particular location and its effects upon man; and third, because culture—as part of the differential that includes nature—is inseparable from the nature that both defines and contributes to its difference, and is seen as having a life of its own rather than an existence that is generated by man. This is not a view that man—who sees himself as the king of culture—is accustomed to adopting; indeed, it is a view that man seems to find most unpalatable.

As the apparent king of culture, man senses a heavy air of determinism in the differential of culture and nature, and inasmuch as any whiff of determinism affects his sense of dignity, he instinctively rebels against the premises inherent in such a view—*determinism*, after all, has been a word laden with pejorative connotations within our language for a long time, even longer than the more readily apparent buzzwords like *capitalism* and *communism*, which in their normal use have really only become subspecies of the word *determinism*. A procapitalist generally uses the word *capitalism* to mean free will while he attaches a heavy sense of determinism to *communism*, just as a procommunist sees capitalism as constituting the worst kind of slavery, though he might well admit to the heavy dose of determinism inherent in the inevitability of the evolution of the masses to their final state. We know that both systems—like any network of relations—have their own kinds of bondage and freedom, and while we might be right in assuming that, historically speaking, capitalism is less of an enslaver than communism, the real problem occurs because we fail to see beyond our own emotions, and hence fail to investigate how our freedoms are established in conjunction with our bondage. *Determinism* is such a powerful word that it can immediately put an end to a conversation—since man's very essence, after all, is freedom, to be placed as a determinist is to be construed as being against man—so one is immediately thrust in with the criminal elements, oppressors, fascists, and any number of other undesirable human types.

The key issue that always gets ignored once one is relegated to the oblivion of the antihuman is the question of whether man is more free by asserting his freedom in opposition to that which could have determinative power over him, or

whether he is more free by first discerning that over which
he can have no power, the "It was" of time. Is man more
determined by attempting to understand those ways in which
he is swept along by the life of the culture or less determined?
Historically speaking, our own epoch has argued that man is
less free to the extent that he considers that which limits him,
and this is most obvious again in the political arena—to assert
the freedom of democracy is to deny determinism; to assert
the values of communism is to concede the bondage and
oppression of human nature. Of course, the communist who
asserts the inevitability of the historical process that will lead
to the dictatorship of the proletariat and the withering away
of the state is arguing that freedom will come from this determinism, but no one who has seen the historical facts of communist societies would readily agree to that. Equally, from
the democratic view, to accept the inevitability of the emergence of man from culture rather than the other way around
is to say the same thing a good communist would, for he does
indeed speak about the inevitability of history. There is a
crucial difference, of course, for to assert the priority of the
culture/nature differential and the "It was" with which it is
bound up is not necessarily to assert that the future bears the
same inevitability as the past, as a Marxist would maintain.
On the contrary, the argument outlined here focuses on learning to accept that which is inevitable, that which is determined, precisely so as to minimize the inevitability of the
future, to make man less determined in his future than he is
now while he asserts his freedom over the past, over culture,
and over nature.

To accept the priority of the culture/nature differential is
simply to concede the obvious, that culture and nature exist
before we do even as we are a part of their history; to accept
their priority means that we can begin to understand the
history of the differential in order better to discern our place
within it; to accept the priority of culture and nature and the
"It was" that asserts the differential is thus to make possible
the questioning of a future that is less inevitable than it would
be if we failed to see ourselves in this light. In accepting the
priority of the differential, one does not deny the effects of

man on it, for even if man is the result of the differential rather than the determiner of it, he still has great effects on both aspects of it. One accepts the differential rather to make man more effective, not less, to make his actions more valuable and less random, to give shape to the ways in which the possibilities of the future can emerge more productively out of the "It was" rather than in simple opposition to it. It is not, as T. S. Eliot said, that only through time is time conquered, for time is *never* conquered, but it is true that only through time is time best understood and put to use. Only through time can man raise the questions of the future that will allow him to escape some of the inevitability of the past.

If we then turn to the inevitabilities inherent in the "It was" of the culture/nature differential, we need to discern what is inevitable in culture and nature and what is not. "Inevitability" in this sense is used in a qualified way, for in one way nothing is inevitable—we could choose to blow up the world, and that would certainly eliminate a great deal of what I shall call the inevitable. I am using the word only to denote that without which it is impossible to think of the continuation of that which is on the planet on which we live. In this sense, for example, both science and technology are inevitable, for we cannot imagine the world without them without at the same time imagining changes so radical that little as we presently find it would be the same—and in any case, to try to imagine the world without science and technology is simply to continue to deny the "It was," to wish it away, to dream of a time before these "corrupting" influences in our lives came to be. The transformations of the earth through which we live our lives have become so connected to science and technology that we must imagine a future with them in it. In the same way, it is not inevitable that man should see himself as having priority over culture and nature, first, because that is a relatively new idea and, second, because the force of the idea has already been irretrievably eroded by the tools of that vision, science and technology. If the force of the tools seems stronger than ever, and if the image that generated the tools has been seriously undermined by them, we might infer that at present the tools are far more inevitable than the image.

But then we must imagine what kind of an image can go along with the tools that have become an essential aspect of man's existence. How is man to continue to maintain his relationship to science and technology now that his image has changed? What inevitabilities are part of the relationship that has been established among these three networks of activity?

One inevitability we confront is the change in the description of the relationship itself. Man is the opening through which culture and nature emerge in their difference, and inasmuch as science and technology are two central aspects of that difference, this means that the questions man asks that allow science and technology to emerge further must be considered in a new light. We can no longer ask the naïve question of what we want to do with science and technology; rather, we need to ask ourselves what questions will allow a place for man, just as we need to ask what questions will allow man, science, and technology to emerge in ways that are consonant with the understanding to which they have already brought us. This means that our questions of science and technology must lead us to ask about the nature of the limit of their background rhythms. Put another way, we need to ask how the differential defines and is defined by the background rhythms of which it is an expression, and we can only do this by seeing the differential and the background rhythms as consonant with each other rather than in opposition. In considering science and technology themselves, we need to ask how to put them to use in ways that work in accord with the background rhythms rather than in opposition to them; we must see them as part of the differential that allows nature to emerge rather than as an attempt to overcome the differential itself and thus put the force of nature out of play. Inasmuch as we can only put the force of nature out of play by using its full force to negate the differential altogether—as in a nuclear explosion that would end the differential by eliminating culture—there seems to be little point in working further against the differential, for striving to oppose it always inevitably brings us back to the inevitability of it.

In short, we must change the nature of the questions we ask of science and technology in order to make them correspond

better to the questioning we have found at the heart of them—
we must begin to see them as processes that open up the
world and define man rather than as instruments of domina-
tion over the inevitabilities we have so strenuously resisted.
To be sure, this mode of questioning has always been at the
heart of science and technology—it has only been our willful
misrepresentations of their processes that has kept us from
seeing it more clearly. But how are we to question science and
technology in ways that more fully bring into the foreground
the limits of the background rhythms they have already
pointed us toward? The most important thing we can do is
simply listen to what they have already told us, for their
insights have brought us face to face with the orientation that
attaches itself to the background. To recognize this is only
to accept what science has already shown us in its various
domains, and without the recognition of where we have come
to as a result of science, we will not be able to ask of it the
questions we need to raise.

From there, perhaps the chief step in our questions toward
science and technology has to come from an awareness of
the middle that marks the horizon of the background. The
problem is not only that the background cannot be properly
measured outside of the middle, though with our propensities
for the short and the long term that is problem enough; the
problem is that we must learn to measure the productivity of
our actions in terms of the middle in relation to the background, for only by doing so can we come to have an adequate
measure for what we choose to do. Again, simply in terms of
our economic language, we tend either to invest in the short
term or the long term, and our questions are dependent on
whether we see things in one or the other of those categories.
To learn to invest in the middle in its relation to the background is thus almost an alien concept to us in all but the
"pure" disciplines that are not directed to the near or far term,
construing their activity rather as a measure of the middle up
against the limits that frame it. But this is seen as a faulty way
of proceeding in more pragmatic domains, in everything from
economics to the use of technology to the way our lives are
marked out. That it is seen as a productive way of proceeding

in pure disciplines is taken to be a mark of their difference rather than as part of a view that would lead to more productive questions in pragmatic areas. The questions of value in any domain emerge out of the middle as it is marked by the limits of the known, and we need to learn to apply this orientation to our questions of science and technology. Put another way, we can say that to frame a question from the middle with its limits inscribed is to begin to consider seriously the consequences of particular questions and the actions that are part of them.

In considering the limit, we must recognize that it no longer follows, for example, that something should be done because it can be done—one must also consider whether it is worth doing so in terms of the limits upon which the question itself is based. The limit introduces a set of values that is missing from our questions when we do not understand the way they are always framed by a context. To take a pragmatic example, the use of nuclear energy today leads us to the question of what to do with the wastes that result from its use. The wastes themselves are part of the limit that the process itself establishes, as many people have pointed out, and the limits of this waste are fairly profound. Given our knowledge of physics and chemistry, there is no known way of neutralizing these wastes—indeed, the possibility for doing so is not even seriously hypothesized at the moment. Because of this limit, and because it is a limit that has already been tested seriously—people have tried to imagine the possibility of neutralizing the waste and what it would take to do so and have come up with nothing—we must assume that we cannot rely on science for a resolution of this problem. It may well some day present us with a solution, but inasmuch as there are no real prospects for it in sight, we cannot readily make decisions on the basis of that possibility.

Without a ready conception of how to neutralize this material—or even a working hypothesis of how it might be done—we must begin to think in terms of containment and storage, and here again we must assume that there will be no easy neutralization solution. The container problem itself is a difficult one, for we have no known, reasonably economical container for these materials that can be counted on over a long period of time to prevent leakage into the environment. And unless we can seriously hypothesize the technology for such a container, we have to act on the premise that nothing of the sort is likely to be forthcoming within the time frame in which it will be required. Talk of burial of these wastes in salt domes and the like seems far too risky given our knowledge of activities inside of the earth and given our relative ignorance of what happens to nuclear wastes when they are placed in this kind of environment. In each case, the limit imposed on the question from the outset cannot be properly addressed, so unless further questions emerge that address seriously the limit of one of these possibilities, it only makes sense not to continue to generate further wastes. To be sure, one can argue that we could simply ship the wastes into outer space, eliminating them from our immediate environment, and there is something appealing to that notion inasmuch as it seems to free man of the problem. It also, unfortunately, bears all too much resemblance to the first man's cultivating the first plot of ground in all of his ignorance of the potential changes he was introducing into the local environment. To begin to use space as a repository for that which we do not know what to do with is merely to perpetuate the kinds of activity that have led to many of the problems we already face. Instead of learning more about the ways in which small changes can have large effects—as shown all too evidently on earth—we choose to apply that understanding only to earth; it is as though outer space somehow exists extrinsic of our world rather than being a part of it. It is not simply that we do not know what the consequences of this action might be for us— outer space is certainly large enough for us to imagine little of consequence happening. It is rather that our present understanding of the world has already shown us the values inherent in that kind of thinking, and the values are not simply a local issue—to choose to thrust our garbage into outer space is to choose a value system that is ultimately pernicious in its consequences, even if it does solve our problem of nuclear waste for the time being.

The arguments that would be raised in opposition to this

analysis of the problem of nuclear waste would doubtless fall along several other lines as well. One of them would be that to deny ourselves the use of a technology like nuclear energy would be to go against the grain of past human endeavors, for man has always inevitably exploited to the limits the potential of his knowledge. Because we have nuclear capabilities we must use them; to do otherwise is to place a limit on human achievement that is absurd and unrealistic. Of course, the same argument would then have to apply to the use of nuclear bombs too, for we could doubtless learn a great deal about the large-scale effects of nuclear activity on a wide range of phenomena if we were to explore that possibility. If we are willing to face the limit of the nuclear bomb, then, there is no reason not to face the limit of the nuclear waste problem, which is clearly at least as potentially damaging in the long run. It is, after all, one of man's capabilities to recognize certain limits as well as to try to extend them, and if this has always been so, there is no reason why it should not apply here.

A collateral position would be the argument from human ingenuity, the first angle of which would point out that man has always been able to come up with resolutions to such dilemmas in the past, so there is no reason to assume he will not be able to do so again. As with the earlier argument, though, this neglects the fact that man has also recognized his limits at times when it was in his interests to do so. The other angle of this argument would be that man is at his most ingenious when he must be, when he is pushed to the edge, so we are again placing limits on man's quest for knowledge. That this may in some cases be true ignores the stakes of the game in this case as well as reinforces a value system that implicitly connects man's ingenuity to a mindless lack of consideration of consequences.

The most powerful arguments against this view, though, are the pragmatic ones. We are said to need nuclear energy in order to continue the growth of our economy and in order to avoid potential threats to that growth from those who control other energy supplies. And once the antigrowth overtones creep in, there is also the implicit argument that one is limiting the future economic well-being of people by arguing that nuclear wastes should not be produced unless there is a reasonable chance something can be done to guarantee their safety. In the meantime, people are feverishly working on this problem in any case, so we must simply go ahead with what we are doing. That the same human ingenuity could be put to work just as forcefully when there are serious economic consequences at stake—instead of simply environmental consequences—seems to be a point that the pragmatic view would choose to overlook. But surely man's ingenuity would work just as well when the consequences were largely economic as it would if the consequences were environmental, and inasmuch as the risk is greater in the environmental domain, involving as it does much more than an economy or even man, it would make much better sense to spur man's ingenuity through means of lesser risk.

The problem with this example, as with any other one of similar intent, is that it is more likely to be seen in terms of the arguments of particular special interest groups. And inasmuch as most of us have, when called upon, fairly strenuous views on this kind of subject when it is brought up, the nature of the argument itself all too easily gets lost. The point here, however, is less to plead a special case than it is to demonstrate how our questions need to be framed in terms of the limits that define our actions and by our understanding of our ability or inability to change or develop the limit. Without such a mode of questioning in every area of our lives, we will simply continue to move heedlessly in the directions our culture has laid out for us. Only by framing our questions in terms of the awareness of their limits can we hope to begin more consciously to shape the way in which we deal with what the culture/nature differential has given us.

For us, it can no longer be a question merely of doing whatever we choose to do; we need to discern what is fitting in terms of the contexts of our actions. We can no longer be the questioner who refuses to consider the value of the question, for we know too much to be able to do so without at the same time recognizing that the one thing we have learned is that all questions have value, and that the value of the question is framed by its limit. The question of value must certainly be raised in the domains of science and technology, for they have become important components of our world— and the components that most obviously affect the world in which we live—but the question must be applied to all other human domains as well, for the networks of our activity are not discrete but interrelated. If we begin most clearly with the question of science and technology, it is only because science and technology have so powerfully framed our need for questions of value through their own inquiries and the consequences of them on our lives. And if we begin with the question of value in science and technology, it is because the results of our questioning will be much more readily apparent within these domains. If we are indeed at a moment in human history when we have more information about the world than ever before—more even than we can begin to know what to do with—then the best thing we can do with that information is to see the very concept of information as the limit of the discursive network. Our quest for knowledge begins as a value-free endeavor, and it achieves its goal when all of man's knowledge has been transformed into information. In the face of the inundation of information, we see its limit as its attempt to purge thought of value at the very moment when value is needed most in order to determine what information is useful and what is not. At that moment, the limit of technology is also present, not only in the guise of the computer that made so much information possible to begin with, but also in the notion of technology itself as something value-free. The limit of technology must then turn to face the same limit that science has already confronted, the return of value by the inevitable reintroduction of man, the return of the question that demarcates man's space as the inevitable emergence of questioning through the differential of culture and nature that makes man possible in the first place. The return of value is not thus an abandonment of science and technology, but rather an acceptance of the full potential of their limits and of the man who is defined through the questions he allows to emerge in the full acceptance of time and its "It was."

8 The Affirmation of Time

We are told that we live in the postmodern era, a period that seems all too often to differ from the modern age only in the degree of its despair. Indeed, in one sense postmodernism can be said to be little more than taking what we have absorbed from the struggles of the moderns and trying to learn to live with it. The heroism of our struggle is characterized by that "trying to learn to live with it," an expression that suggests we have arrived at certain conclusions about the nature of our world and are now trying to face the consequences, albeit most reluctantly. The conclusion that seems paramount in this view is the inherent meaninglessness of the world and our actions within it—the irony of absurdity still dominates our thought like a gray cloud that will not go away. The absurdity of the postmodern condition is framed by three general principles: (1) an attempt to live with our inability to transcend our world; (2) an attempt to accept the consequence that therefore no values are transcendent, which leads us to the false conclusion that everything is valueless; and (3) an attempt to accept the burdens of the individual in the face of these absurdities. Phrased that way, there seems to be little difference between the modern era and the postmodern one. There is, perhaps, a larger share of despair now, and a serious postmodern would also argue that the individual himself has disappeared along with the possibility of transcendence and transcendental values, but still no one very seriously wishes to give up the individual as a lost cause, no one really wants to accept the end of the individual as we have known him—to do so seems somehow to negate the greatest of things we have hoped for.

Nevertheless, it is also the case that our refusal to give up our sacred sense of the individual generates the despair and absurdity of our world, for it is only absurd when seen through the eyes of an individual who knows there is no longer any place for his conception of individuality in the world. It is the presence of the sacred self that makes the world absurd, just as it is the self's presence that makes values impossible, yet, though we claim to have learned from the moderns, we have failed to learn the lessons of the individual. We have preferred instead to live with our pain rather than reject the primary source of it. So our struggle becomes heroic because of our resistance to that negation of what is most dear to our hearts. In so resisting what we see as a void that results from the end of the individual, we have simply allowed the sense of void to saturate everything.

Yet in spite of our despair at the void, it is increasingly difficult to hear what the existentialists have called an authentic voice. It is hard to find a questioner who so attentively listens to his questions in the way that Nietzsche or Heidegger did. We have spawned instead a generation of declaimers who hurl their words into the abyss in a great act of defiance, but those who would listen to the echo of the words seem hard to find. It is equally difficult to locate a thinker who, like Nietzsche, is willing to face again and again the limits of his thought, who is willing to bear the thought that marks and gives shape to that which has led up to it. We have found instead a generation of writers devoted to the destruction of the limit, writers who sniff out the limit like trained dogs and then proceed to attack with all the ferocity they can muster, ignoring the fact that the limit remains a limit after the attack. And when it comes to probing the difference of difference that was papered over through the introduction of the individual, no one has readily taken up Freud's call with the seriousness he was able to bring to the inquiry.

It is not that we have failed to learn anything of value in the past fifty years, for a great deal has been done. It is rather that we have devoted ourselves to ignoring the key thoughts of Nietzsche, Heidegger, and Freud even as they have come to be construed as the iconic figures of our time, and we have done so by misconstruing the value of their work as residing in the opening of the void. We have continued to think at the void because we find Nietzsche himself to be waiting there along with Heidegger and Freud. And in reading them in this way, we have shown our thorough lack of attentiveness to their thought. That the presence of the void can be seen in their work is not to be doubted; after all, their writing occurs in the face of a world view of fullness and transcendence, and to arrive at the point where fullness and transcendence are no longer possible is to feel the force of the abyss opening up before them—the void is present in their work in the face of a fullness they can no longer find. But the void is also an openness to them, a region of possibility that is not based on negation but rather on facing the possibilities inherent in what is, and we seem to have misplaced the sense of openness that is also in their work. We are still reading them in terms of the fullness they called into question, and as long as we do so, we shall find only the abyss and shall confine ourselves to the pursuit of absurdity.

If we are to begin to see the postmodern era in other terms, in terms of the possibilities it presents us, we need to focus on the point of intersection of Nietzsche, Heidegger, and Freud, and that point comes together in Nietzsche's thought of the eternal return, Heidegger's thought of the difference of difference, and Freud's thought of the death instinct. We have met at this point before, but always only to see the negativity in it—the eternal return as a repetition of the same, the difference of difference as the infinite deferral of our desire, and the death instinct as the manifestation of the repetition compulsion that dominates our lives. We have learned these lessons all too well, but we have forgotten that for Nietzsche, Heidegger, and Freud, these moments of negation were presented as moments of openness, as moments when the eternal return, the difference of difference, and the death instinct could be faced in order to lead to their own differences. The eternal return had to be accepted in order to overcome our revulsion against time and the spirit of revenge that followed from our revulsion; the difference of difference had to be faced so that our questions could be framed in the openness the difference provided rather than through the attempt to close up the difference through our assertions; the death instinct had to be confronted in order to overcome the repetition compulsion that dominated our actions. Each of these thoughts is a different expression of the same human dilemma, and we need to deal with the thoughts precisely because they keep us from avoiding the dilemma we do not want to see—only by facing it could Nietzsche, Heidegger, and Freud hope to overcome the dominance of the void in our lives. The reintroduction of the recursive in their thought comes when they turn to these dilemmas and refuse to ignore them; the moment of difference comes when they refuse to return to the repetition compulsion of the discursive that would allow them to avoid arriving where their thought has taken them. And that refusal to return to the discursive is what continues to mark their difference from us, for we are willing to follow them up to this point, yet unwilling to see the possibilities they have opened up in the process. We are still lamenting what we have seen, and our cries have grown so loud that we fail to notice the opening that is present.

Nietzsche, Heidegger, and Freud brought us to the limit, and they showed us how it provided an openness rather than a closure; they showed us how openness itself is based on the limit, how the question always only opens by limiting. Equally, the limit of difference we had avoided and chosen to see as that which foreclosed all possibilities was shown to be the opening through which any possibilities appeared in the first place. Yet we have continued to see closure in limit just as we fail to notice how the grafting of difference is that which opens. That similar conclusions about the limit and about difference were also to be found in our sciences and became the very root of our technology was beside the point, for those domains did not explicitly force us to accept the philosophical consequences—physicists could go about their work through the limit of difference, and what they achieved did not have to be seen as based on the limit of difference, even though it was. Technology could do the same, but its products did not force us to consider the implications inherent in them. Philosophy, however, speaks to man, not the universe or products, so it is much harder to deal with the same questions there precisely because that is where we have to deal with them. So we have yet to learn to live with that which we already know; we have yet to escape the repetition compulsion of escape.

Nevertheless, when we turn to philosophy, we must ask ourselves the same questions, and sooner or later we shall have to listen to the answers that come forth. We can begin by lauding—as Nietzsche and Heidegger did—the essentially aesthetic attitude toward the world that humans have, but we must go on from there to consider what this means for the true and the good. If we wish to argue that our aesthetic viewpoint is the negation of the true and the good, we have failed fully to understand the implications of the aesthetic. In so doing, we are only following the lead of Schiller, who saw the virtue of the aesthetic in the fact that it negated the true and the good, which he saw as discursive, in contrast to the recursivity of the aesthetic. But if we begin within the aesthetic and never escape from it, then the true and the good must also be recursive. Again, our thought has led us to this point, but we have interpreted this to mean that therefore the true and the good do not in fact exist. This is the moment when the absurd enters the scene and our despair beckons, even if we choose joyously to affirm the absurdity of an aesthetic devoid of the true and the good.

Nietzsche and Heidegger, however, took a different route. Instead of denying the true and the good because discursivity had been overturned, they showed how the true and the good were always recursive and demonstrated how all of our attempts to make them discursive had failed. Acceptance of the recursive does not lead to the elimination of the true and the good—the discursive attempted to do that in the guise of value-free inquiry and failed. Rather, acceptance leads to the reassertion of the true and the good through their essential connection to the aesthetic. They, too, are marked by the limit; they too can only be based on an acceptance of time and its "It was"; but they are only possible in the first place because they are bound to that limit. Thus, they become what they always were, the coordinates that mark out the limit of our questions through their difference, the differences that allow us to frame our questions in the first place. Our revulsion against the "It was" is thus based on our unwillingness to see in it what is always there, the recursive tendencies of the true and the good.

Our revulsion against time is also based on the power the past has over us and on the finitude that is finally marked by our own end, and in this sense the dread of having to submit to the "It was" becomes still more powerful. Ultimately, however, we have come to see how the "It was" has a greater power over us if we attempt to negate it—we only strengthen its hold through our repetition compulsions and through our deliberate forgetfulness. The more strenuously we fight against it, the more insistently the background limit of time reasserts itself—it returns to our view whether we want it to or not, and each return marks a limit that can either be ignored or worked through. We have certainly tried to ignore or fight against the limits of time, but perhaps we have come to the point where we are ready to accept the limit as something through which we can constructively order our lives rather than ordering them through negation. Perhaps we have arrived at the moment where man is capable of facing the dread of the eternal return and learning to live through its difference.

Heidegger was fond of saying that man is a question, that his role in the world as questioner, as the one who responds to the openness of the query, makes him the question that is posed to the world at the same time that he is in question himself. To see man in this way is to place him under the dominance of the question, and it is also, if we are fully to accept the role, to place him under the dominance of time that he must always ultimately accept, and we have not accustomed ourselves to a view of man in subordination to anything, much less under the sway of time that emerges through the question. From another perspective, though, a great many of man's struggles over the millennia have been carried out in an attempt to overcome this or that element of his world that he felt subordinate to, and after each struggle the sense of subordination remained, for in part what was being fought against was the force of time. In the meantime, we have grown quite comfortable with the role of man as opposer, man the denier, even as we have come to see that what he opposes most is his own nature, his connection to time and the limit. But it may be that neither man nor the world can afford for too much longer to live with man the opposer. It may be time for us most fully to recognize the limit of our lives and the time to which that limit binds us. It may be time, finally, for us to learn to live with the "It was" of which we are a part and willingly fully occupy our space in the world at the openness of the question that allows us and our world to emerge into that of which we are most fully capable.

Works Cited

Works Cited

Derrida, Jacques. "Structure, Sign, and Play in the Discourse of the Human Sciences." In *The Structuralist Controversy*. Eds. Richard Macksey and Eugenio Donato. Baltimore: Johns Hopkins University Press, 1972. 247–65.

Freud, Sigmund. *Beyond the Pleasure Principle*. Trans. James Strachey. New York: W. W. Norton, 1961.

Heidegger, Martin. "The Origin of the Work of Art." In *Poetry, Language, Thought*. Trans. Albert Hofstadter. New York: Harper and Row, 1971. 15–88.

———. "The Word of Nietzsche." In *The Question Concerning Technology and Other Essays*. Trans. William Lovitt. New York: Harper and Row, 1977. 53–114.

———. *What Is Called Thinking?* Trans. Fred D. Wieck and J. Glenn Gray. New York: Harper and Row, 1972.

Nietzsche, Friedrich. *Beyond Good and Evil*. Trans. Walter Kaufmann. New York: Random House, Vintage Books, 1966.

———. *On the Genealogy of Morals*. Trans. Walter Kaufmann. New York: Random House, Vintage Books, 1967.

———. *The Gay Science*. Trans. Walter Kaufmann. New York: Random House, Vintage Books, 1974.

James S. Hans is Associate Professor of English at Wake Forest University. His previous books are *The Play of the World* and *Imitation and the Image of Man*. He has also published numerous essays on modern and contemporary American literature and contemporary literary theory and Continental philosophy.